Kurdistan Regional Government
Ministry of Planning • Ministry of Education

Improving Technical Vocational Education and Training in the Kurdistan Region—Iraq

Sponsored by the Kurdistan Regional Government

Louay Constant
Shelly Culbertson
Cathleen Stasz
Georges Vernez

RAND EDUCATION

The research described in this report was sponsored by the Kurdistan Regional Government and was conducted in RAND Education, a unit of the RAND Corporation.

Library of Congress Control Number: 2014936284

ISBN: 978-0-8330-8071-4

Cover images used with permission. Upper left photo courtesy of Howard J. Shatz, all others Thinkstock.

RAND OFFICES

SANTA MONICA, CA • WASHINGTON, DC

PITTSBURGH, PA • NEW ORLEANS, LA • JACKSON, MS • BOSTON, MA

CAMBRIDGE, UK • BRUSSELS, BE

Preface

The Kurdistan Region—Iraq is enjoying rapid economic growth, but the lack of skilled workers may constrain continued growth. As part of its sweeping efforts to transform and grow the region's education system, the Kurdistan Regional Government asked the RAND Corporation to assess its Technical and Vocational Education and Training (TVET) system. This report fulfills that request and recommends measures to increase TVET quality and access.

This report was prepared by RAND Education for the Kurdistan Region—Iraq. The findings of this study should be of interest to persons involved in education in the Kurdistan Region—Iraq as well as to others elsewhere involved in technical and vocational education and training.

The principal investigators of this work are Georges Vernez and Shelly Culbertson. Dr. Vernez may be contacted by email at vernez@rand.org or by phone at 310-393-0411, extension 6211, and Ms. Culbertson may be contacted by email at shellyc@rand.org. For more information on RAND Education, contact the Director, Darleen Opfer, who can be reached by email at dopfer@rand.org; by phone at 310-393-0411, extension 4926; or by mail at RAND Corporation, 1776 Main Street, P.O. Box 3138, Santa Monica, CA 90407-2138.

More information about RAND is available at www.rand.org.

Contents

Figures

Tables

Summary

The Kurdistan Region—Iraq (KRI) is enjoying rapid economic growth, creating many new jobs. Many of these jobs require a solid education and technical skills. The ability of the KRI and its government to provide needed skills to the labor force will partly determine how rapidly the region's economy will grow.

As part of its sweeping efforts to transform and grow the KRI's education system, the Kurdistan Regional Government (KRG) asked the RAND Corporation to assess its Technical and Vocational Education and Training (TVET) system. While the KRG has expanded opportunities for post-secondary technical and university education, secondary-level vocational education has lagged. This has left many who cannot or do not want to pursue post-secondary education without the necessary skills that would enable them to contribute to the KRI's evolving labor market and economy. In response, some local and foreign companies have hired foreign workers when they cannot find local graduates with the right skills. Even though the KRI is establishing three new vocational education centers, more work is needed to address current shortcomings and future needs.

To assess the current TVET system in the KRI and make recommendations for its improvement, we undertook several tasks. These included a literature review on effective TVET systems, analyses of secondary data on TVET programs in the region, interviews with leaders and staff of the KRI ministries responsible for TVET, case studies of TVET systems in other countries, and a survey of KRI employers on their workforce needs. We present our findings in four sections: KRI's current TVET system and its structure; labor and skill needs in the KRI economy; international TVET policies and practices; and recommendations for improvements.

Findings

The KRI's Current TVET Preparation Is Inadequate

The current TVET system has secondary, post-secondary, and adult components, each administered by a different government ministry. Upon completion of compulsory basic education through the 9th grade, students may enroll in college-preparatory programs or vocational education, or enter the labor force. Most enroll in college-preparatory courses, while a large number enter the labor force. Only a small number—about 2,000 of more than 80,000 in one recent cohort—enter secondary-level vocational education. Reasons for this include the perceived poor quality of secondary-level TVET; the inability of most graduates to find jobs; the inability to matriculate from secondary-level TVET to post-secondary education; and a weak relationship between TVET programs and labor market demand. Post-secondary technical education has a better reputation and higher participation. Indeed, enrollment in post-secondary TVET programs has increased sharply in recent years, while enrollment in secondary-level vocational education and training has stagnated.

The current TVET system has several additional shortcomings. Coordination across the three components of the TVET system is infrequent. Occupational offerings are too few and are not driven by labor market demands. Curricula in all three components are often obsolete and provide for insufficient practical experience. And there are no uniform TVET qualification standards by which employers can judge whether the program will adequately prepare students for employment.

TVET Can Help Prepare for Current and Future Jobs

Expected employment growth in the KRI economy is likely to be in the service, wholesale, and transportation sectors—and individuals with a secondary-level vocational education could fill many of these jobs. Nearly three-fourths of jobs in the private sector are in occupations—services and sales, skilled agricultural, craft and related trades, plant, machine operators and assemblers, and clerical support positions—for which secondary vocational education and training may provide adequate preparation. Yet more than one-third of employers we asked said that secondary-school graduates, both general and vocational, were ill prepared to join the workforce. They identified a lack of appropriate technical skills and of work experience as major barriers to hiring locally. Other skill deficits included foreign languages and use of information technology, as well as "soft skills" such as communication, dealing with customers, and teamwork. Occupations for which employers had particular difficulties hiring included technicians; process plant and machine operators; sales and customer service; and some skilled trades.

International Practices Provide Lessons for Improving TVET in the KRI

Our literature review and country case studies identified many practices that provide lessons for improving TVET in the KRI. To ensure relevance to the labor market, TVET systems typically align programs with labor market needs, coordinate programs at the secondary level and post-secondary level, and incorporate input from social partners such as employers, unions, and industry organizations. While most nations rely on school-based vocational and technical education programs at the secondary level, their curricula also include opportunities for workplace learning or internships. Some countries have formal apprenticeships, which combine school-based learning with paid work and in which contracts between student and employer help to ensure quality. Workplace learning is seen in most countries as a key feature of effective programs. Curricula include both general and vocational subjects in order to better prepare students for post-secondary studies or for career changes over their working lives. TVET systems in other nations also include guidance and counseling for students to help them learn about labor-market options and the training needed for them. Many also require TVET teachers to have at least a bachelor's degree in addition to practical experience in relevant occupations.

Recommendations

The findings suggest several recommendations for improving TVET in the KRI, particularly at the secondary level. Rather than implementing all of these at once, we suggest three phases to allow for measured implementation.

In the short term, the KRI should pursue several strategies to set up the system and with consideration of their ongoing TVET reforms. These include:

- collecting and analyzing data about labor market needs
- establishing governance and supporting structures for technical vocational education and training
- setting the vision and goals for the TVET system
- initiating the design of occupational standards, curricula, and student qualification requirements, with involvement of employers and other social partners
- incorporating soft skills and practical learning into the school-based curriculum through workshops and internships
- setting requirements for TVET teachers.

In the medium term, policymakers should:

- draft and enact TVET legislation
- align secondary and tertiary TVET curricula to support transitions for students seeking further education
- expand vocational program offerings in new occupations, in consultation with employers
- design and pilot formal apprenticeship programs.

Over the long term, policymakers should:

- expand apprenticeship programs if pilot efforts are successful
- establish a process to review occupational course offerings and vocational education and training programs
- design and establish guidance and counseling programs for students
- develop means to better prepare TVET teachers and counselors.

Implementing these recommendations can help the Kurdistan Region—Iraq support its rapid economic growth through a vocational education and training system that would better align with its needs and also reflect international best practices.

Acknowledgements

We are grateful to the Kurdistan Regional Government (KRG) for supporting this research. We are especially grateful for the advice and support provided by Their Excellencies Dr. Ali Sindi, Minister of Planning, and Mr. Safeen M. Dizayee, Minister of Education, during the first part of our project, and Dr. Asmat Muhamad Khalid, Minister of Education, during the second part of our project. Although we have received information, support, and feedback from numerous KRG officials, we are particularly indebted to Mr. Zagros Fatah Siwaily, Director General of the Capital Investment Budget and former Director General of Development Coordination and Cooperation, Ministry of Planning; Mr. Yosuif Othman Yosuif, Director General, Ministry of Education; Mr. Ahmed Smail Rahman, Director General, Ministry of Education; Mr. Yousif Abdullah M., Director, Ministry of Education; Ms. Dastan A. Ali, Senior Coordinator, Ministry of Education; Mr. Haji Rasul Ali, Director General, Ministry of Labor and Social Affairs; Dr. Kawther Aziz Galaly, President of Foundation of Technical Education, Erbil; and Dr. Nasih Othman, Vice President of Foundation of Technical Education, Sulaimaniya, Ministry of Higher Education and Scientific Research.

We would also like to thank the Ministry of Planning staff, includingMr. Worya Mahmood, Mr. Hoshyar Aziz, Mr. Omar Abit, and Mr. Muhammad A. Ahmed, who facilitated our work in the Kurdistan Region—Iraq.

The many dedicated Kurdistan Region—Iraq technical vocational education and training administrators, principals, professors, and teachers who shared their experience and concerns with us also deserve special recognition.

At RAND, we are grateful to Drs. Jill Luoto and Howard Shatz for their work on the development of the survey of employers and analysis of the data and to Beth Katz who participated in the country case studies of technical and vocational education and training systems. We are also indebted to Dr. Haitham Numan of ASHARQ Co. Ltd. and his staff for the fielding of the employer survey.

Finally, we thank Drs. Marlaine Lockheed and Robert Bozick for their reviews. They made many suggestions that significantly improved this report. Also, many thanks to Ms. Donna White, who typed the final version of this report.

Abbreviations

BIBB	Federal Institute for Vocational Education and Training
BTP	Brevet de Technicien Professionnel
DG	Director General
E-TVET	employment and technical and vocational education and training
ILO	International Labour Organization
IQD	Iraqi dinars
ISCED	International Standard Classification of Education
IT	information technology
IVET	initial vocational education and training
KRG	Kurdistan Regional Government
KRI	Kurdistan Region–Iraq
KRLFS	Kurdistan Region Labor Force Survey
KRSO	Kurdistan Region Statistics Office
MOE	Ministry of Education
MOHESR	Ministry of Higher Education and Scientific Research
MOLSA	Ministry of Labor and Social Affairs
NGO	nongovernmental organization
OECD	Organization for Economic Cooperation and Development
PE	physical education
TVET	technical and vocational education and training
UNESCO	United Nations Educational, Scientific, and Cultural Organization
VET	vocational education and training

CHAPTER ONE

Introduction

A skilled and well-educated labor force is crucial for every country's economic development. As the Kurdistan Region–Iraq's (KRI's) economy is developing rapidly, it is creating jobs that require a solid education and technical skills. Providing the KRI's labor force with needed skills will be a priority for the Kurdistan Regional Government (KRG).

Over the past few years, the KRG has launched an ambitious reform of basic and secondary education to increase its quality and has expanded opportunities for tertiary technical and university education (Vernez, Culbertson, and Constant, 2012). But expansion of secondary vocational education has lagged, leaving many students who cannot or do not want to pursue post-secondary education without the necessary preparation to compete in the KRI's evolving labor market and contribute to its economy. Enrollment in KRI's secondary vocational education has diminished in recent years, and graduates often have difficulty finding employment because their programs have not given them the skills required by employers. Unemployment among youth (aged 15 to 24) is currently 18 percent. At the same time, employers complain that graduates from local general and vocational educational institutions do not possess the skills they need, including numeracy, writing, information technology (IT) and hands-on technical skills. As a result, firms are said to resort to hiring foreign labor whenever they cannot find local graduates with the right combination of skills. The extent of the skill gap, however, remains to be quantified.

As part of its sweeping efforts to transform and grow the KRI's education system, the KRG asked the RAND Corporation to assess its Technical and Vocational Education and Training (TVET) system. This report fulfills that request and recommends measures to increase accessibility and quality of TVET.[1] We begin by providing background about the KRI, a brief overview of its education and TVET systems, and a description of the study methods.

Background

The KRI is a semi-autonomous region in northern Iraq and bordering Iran to the east, Turkey to the north, and Syria to the west. It is comparable in size to the Netherlands or Switzerland. The KRI is divided into three governorates—Duhok, Erbil, and Sulaimaniya—each with a capital city of that name (Figure 1.1). Each of these governorates is divided into districts, for

[1] In an earlier report, we provided an assessment of the status of the KRI's basic and secondary education and made recommendations to improve its quality (Vernez, Culbertson, and Constant, 2012).

Figure 1.1
Current Kurdistan Regional Government's Geographical Boundaries

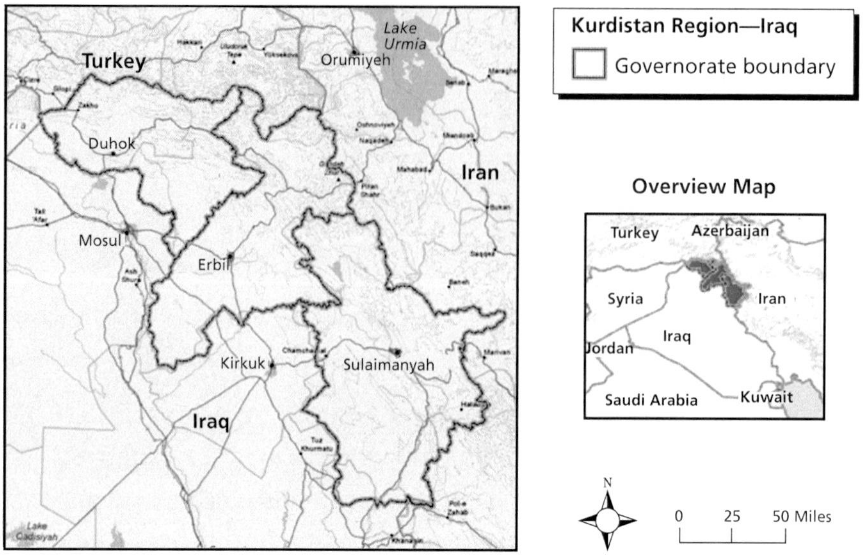

RAND *MG1140-1.1*

a total of 33 districts. Each district is divided into sub-districts. Each district and sub-district has a district center.

Economy, Population, and Workforce

The KRI economy is dominated by government employment, construction, wholesale and retail, and agriculture. It also has a growing oil industry. The relative security and stability of the region has allowed the KRG to improve the region's housing, transportation, and power infrastructure, and to upgrade and expand services in recent years.[2] The KRG currently receives 17 percent of Iraqi government revenues after deductions for defense and other nationwide services.[3]

The KRI had an estimated population of 5 million in 2012.[4] The population of the region is young, with 50 percent under the age of 20. Illiteracy is relatively high: 11 percent of males and 27 percent of females aged 20 to 29 are illiterate, as are 28 percent of the male population and 43 percent of the female population aged 30 or older.[5]

Among the adult population aged 15 and older, participation of the adult population in the labor force is low, at about 38 percent. About two-thirds of men are in the labor force, but

---

[2] Since 1991, about two-thirds of the 4,500 villages destroyed by Saddam Hussein's regime have been reconstructed.

[3] This percentage is presumably equivalent to the share of the KRI population in the total population of Iraq. However, the actual relative population size of the KRI remains unknown because there has not been a national census conducted in decades.

[4] This estimate is based on the Kurdistan Region Labor Force Survey (KRLFS) of 2012. No census of the population has been made in recent times.

[5] Illiteracy is defined as not being able to read and write in one's primary language.

only 12 percent of women are. These gender differences are mirrored in unemployment rates. Male unemployment is about five percent, while female unemployment is four times higher at 20 percent. Joblessness among youths is more than twice the 7 percent unemployment rate of the entire population.

About half of the employed population work for the government. Thirteen percent of employed persons work in construction; another 11 percent in wholesale and retail trade; six percent in agriculture; six percent in transport and communications; and one percent in manufacturing (KRLFS, 2012).

Education

Three ministries and some private establishments provide education in the KRI. The Ministry of Education (MOE) is responsible for basic and secondary education, including secondary vocational education. The Ministry of Higher Education and Scientific Research (MOHESR) is responsible for tertiary two-year and four-year technical and academic education as well as for post-graduate education. And the Ministry of Labor and Social Affairs (MOLSA) is responsible for post-secondary non-tertiary adult training.

Basic and Secondary Education

The Ministry of Education introduced a number of major K–12 education reforms in the 2008–09 school year. Education had been compulsory through grade 6, but is now compulsory through grade 9. A new, more rigorous curriculum has been implemented across the grades. The three previous levels of primary (grades 1 through 6), intermediate (grades 7 through 9), and secondary (grades 10 through 12) have been restructured into two levels, basic (grades 1 to 9) and secondary (grades 10 to 12). At the secondary level, students may choose one of two tracks, vocational or preparatory education, with most students choosing the latter.

Teachers are required to complete higher levels of education than before the 2008 reforms, with new teachers now required to have bachelor's degrees. Previously, teachers could have degrees from teaching institutes, which were five-year programs that started after grade 9 and continued through to the equivalent of the second year of tertiary education. The MOE also instituted policies to reduce the rate at which students are held back in the early grades and instituted two new national exams.

In 2011–12, there were 356 kindergarten schools, 4,598 basic schools, 816 secondary schools, and 32 secondary-level vocational schools. Altogether, these schools served some 1.5 million students, an increase from 1.1 million in 2004–05 (Figure 1.2), and were taught by 98,000 teachers, an increase from 60,000 in 2004–05. The average student-teacher ratio is now about 15 to 1. School infrastructure has not kept pace with growth. Schools at all levels are crowded, in poor repair, and often operate in double shifts.[6] This rapid growth of the number of students in the school system has put increasing pressure on the limited numbers of school buildings and trained teachers.

---

[6] For a recent assessment of basic and secondary education in the KRI, see Vernez, Culbertson, and Constant (2012).

Higher Education

Higher education also has grown rapidly in recent years (Figure 1.2). Before 2004, there was one public university in each of the capitals of the three governorates; since then, an additional seven public universities have been established, one each in the district centers of Koya, Soran, Garmyan, Halabja, Zakho, and Raparin, along with a second one in Erbil. Several private universities also have opened since 2003, including the American University in Sulaimaniya and six such institutions in Erbil. The MOHESR also administers 23 two-year technical institutes and two newly established four-year technical colleges.

In 2012, 90,000 students attended public universities and technical institutes and colleges, an increase from 55,000 in 2006. Students in public universities and technical education are assigned to institutions and academic and technical programs based on their scores on the KRG's secondary-school ministerial exam. According to the hierarchy of professions and academic specialties, the highest scorers are assigned to medical schools, the second-highest to engineering schools, and so on. Students assigned to technical education are among the lowest-scoring.

Adult Training

Vocational skills training for individuals aged 18 or older who did not complete compulsory education or who want to obtain some professional training is provided in three training centers operated by MOLSA. Because of space and resources constraints, these centers enroll only a small number of adults at a time.

Figure 1.2
Student Enrollment, by Education Level, 2007–2012

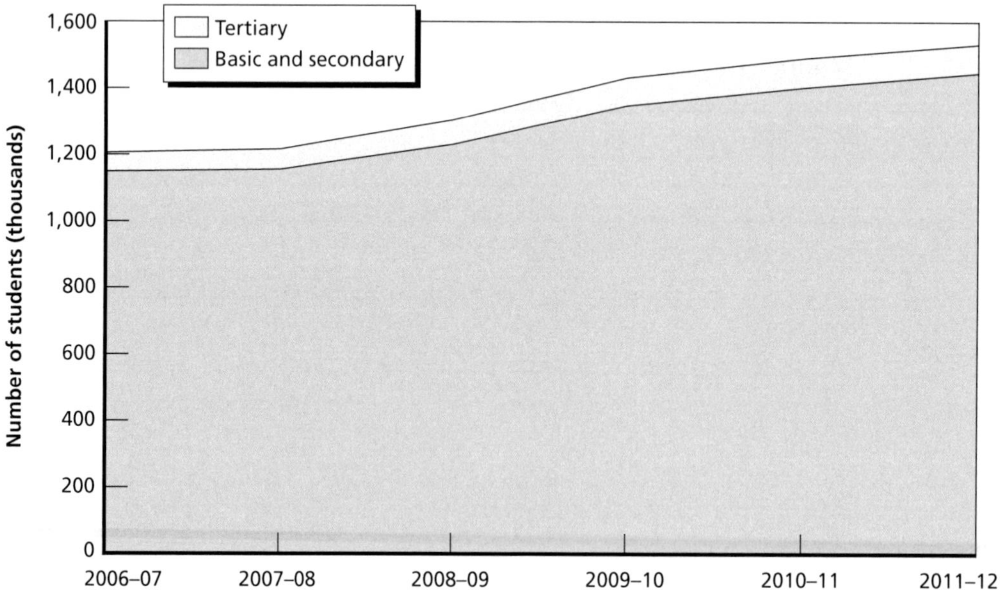

SOURCES: MOE and MOHESR.

RAND *RR277-1.2*

Study Methods

To assess the TVET system and support the KRG planning effort that is already underway to improve quality of and access to the system, we undertook several related tasks. We analyzed secondary data on TVET programs in the KRI, interviewed leaders and staff of the KRI ministries responsible for the TVET system, visited TVET schools and institutes, administered a survey of KRI employers on workforce needs, reviewed the TVET literature, and undertook case studies of TVET systems in other countries.

Secondary Data Analysis

We obtained and analyzed data from the MOE's 2007–08 and 2010–11 surveys of schools and from the 2012 KRLFS. The MOE's survey of schools is administered annually to all kindergarten, basic, and secondary school principals. It collects information on enrollment, student gender and age, teacher education and gender, and student performance for each grade and type of school. We used this information to describe enrollment trends.

The KRLFS was administered to a random sample of 7,000 households from across the KRI representing all governorates and districts, both urban and rural. Responses were weighted to be representative of the KRI's population by region. It collected data on household members' education, employment status, wages and benefits, and other general characteristics.[7] We used this information to analyze the distribution of employees by economic sector and type of occupations as well as the range of jobs whose skill requirements may be met by TVET programs.

We also obtained administrative data from each of the three ministries providing TVET education, including information on curricula, occupational programs offered, student enrollment, and student admission and qualification requirements.

On-Site Interviews with Relevant Officials

We made several trips to Kurdistan, spending a total of seven weeks in the region. We used these trips to conduct 27 interviews with the director general, directors, and staffs from all three ministries and from all three governorates providing and overseeing TVET programs. We used these interviews to gather information on the perceived strengths and weaknesses of the TVET programs and their institutional setup, teacher requirements, and relationships with one another and with the private sector. We also conducted 30 interviews and focus groups with a convenience sample of medium- and large-sized employers across sectors and with TVET staffs to identify missing skills among TVET graduates that may affect employers' plans for growth. These interviews were designed to complement as well as provide more in-depth information on skill demanded than was possible to collect in our survey of employers (see below).

TVET's School and Institute Visits, Focus Groups, and Interviews

We visited five MOE vocational schools, three MOHESR technical institutes and one technical college, and one MOLSA training center. During these visits, we toured the facilities and interviewed the head of each facility, instructional staff, and students. In several visits, we conducted focus groups with teachers and students. These visits provided information on the physical characteristics and conditions of the facilities and workshop equipment and on

---

[7] For more details on the KRLFS, see Abramzon et al. (2013).

the strengths and weaknesses of the curricula, teacher preparation, and links with the labor market. We also obtained information on student views of their program of studies and prospect for progression in their studies and employment.

Survey of Business Establishments

We surveyed 360 private sector employers randomly selected from the 2011–2012 Kurdistan Region Companies Directory, exclusive of firms in the agricultural sector and with less than five employees, and complemented with firms from the KRSO's 2009 enumeration of business establishments.[8] The sample was stratified by governorate (Erbil, Sulaimaniya, and Duhok), sector (mining and manufacturing, infrastructure, and services and professions), and size (small, medium, and large). Firms were sampled until our target of 50 firms in each stratum was reached. The Kurdistan Region Companies Directory is a listing of formal businesses assembled by the Kurdistan Region Chamber of Commerce and Industry.[9] Firm managers or their representatives were interviewed in person, and after making up to three attempts to contact sampled companies, we achieved a high response rate of 90 percent. The sample was weighted to more closely reflect the population of firms in the KRI.

The survey collected quantitative data on current employees, expected new hires over the next two years, skills requirements by type of job, experience with graduates from KRI's TVET programs, and training provided by firms to employees. RAND designed the survey instruments and sampling strategy while ASHARQ, an Iraqi survey firm, collected the data.

Literature Review and Case Studies

We reviewed relevant written documents from the MOE, MOHESR, and MOLSA within the KRI and from the United Nations Educational, Scientific, and Cultural Organization (UNESCO) and other organizations (e.g., European Training Funds, Organization for Economic Cooperation and Development [OECD], World Bank) elsewhere who have reported on TVET issues in the KRI or the Middle East. Our review of literature on effective TVET systems paid particular attention to reviews and assessments made across countries. We sought examples of practices in a range of countries, mostly but not exclusively from members of the OECD, on which there is extensive literature regarding TVET. We also reviewed the literature on employer demand for skills, focusing on studies that had gathered data directly from employers. See references at the end of this report for more details on the range of studies and documents reviewed.

We conducted detailed and comparative reviews of the TVET systems in six countries—Germany, Finland, Jordan, Korea, Tunisia, and Turkey—to obtain more information on similarities and differences in TVET policies and practices. We selected these countries to represent a variety of highly regarded TVET models in developed and developing countries. For each country, we reviewed their TVET system components, pathways, student admis-

---

[8] We intended initially to use the KRSO's 2009 enumeration of establishments as our primary sampling frame but encountered difficulties locating establishments during the fielding using the address information it contained. Updating the 2009 enumeration of establishments was beyond our resources, and we had to turn to using primarily the 2011–2012 Kurdistan Region Companies Directory as our primary sampling frame. About 83 percent of our sample firms came from the latter source and the remainder came from the 2009 enumaration of establishments.

[9] Firms with four or fewer employees were not included in the sample because most are family enterprises, and we expect that future local and foreign investments and growth will take place in larger-size firms.

sion requirements, student guidance and counseling, curricula, occupational programs, governance, finance, quality assurance, teacher qualification requirements, and occupation and skill forecasting capabilities and utilization. A separate report was prepared for each country.

Outline of the Report

In Chapter Two, we provide a qualitative and quantitative description of TVET programs in the KRI and of ongoing plans for improvement. Chapter Three discusses the range of technical and other skills that employers in the KRI say they need and identifies skills gaps for recent graduates of TVET and educational programs. Chapter Four provides an overview of why countries invest in vocational education and how TVET programs are structured within the broader education system. We also describe similarities and differences in TVET policies and practices in other countries, particularly in vocational education and training at the secondary level. Finally, in Chapter Five, we offer recommendations and a roadmap for expanding and improving the effectiveness of TVET preparation in the KRI.

CHAPTER TWO

The KRI's Current TVET System

In this chapter, we first provide an overview of the TVET system in the KRI. We then discuss the characteristics of its secondary, tertiary, and adult components, including their institutional supporting arrangements, curricula, occupational offerings, and teacher qualification requirements. Finally, we review ongoing and planned initiatives for growth and improvement of the system before summarizing our findings and their implications.

Overview

Three ministries provide TVET, targeting different populations of students:

- **The Ministry of Education** (MOE) offers secondary students (grades 10 through 12) *vocational education* (ISCED 3).[1] The 32 secondary-level vocational schools enrolled 8,600 students in 2011–12, or 3 percent of all secondary-school students.
- **The Ministry of Higher Education and Scientific Research** (MOHESR) provides *technical education* in 23 two-year *technical institutes* and two four-year *technical colleges* to graduates from secondary schools (ISCED 5). These schools enrolled about 30,000 students in 2012, accounting for 33 percent of post-secondary students.
- **The Ministry of Labor and Social Affairs** (MOLSA) provides *vocational* skills training in three training centers to adults aged 18 or older who did not complete compulsory education or want to obtain some professional training (ISCED 4). Less than 1 percent of adults each year participate in such training.

Figure 2.1 illustrates the flow of students through the various components of the TVET and general education system, using the cohort of students that completed basic education in 2007 and who are expected to complete four years of university in 2014.[2] The bottom of the figure shows that 84,839 students completed compulsory basic education (that is, education through the 9th grade) in 2007. Of these, most (58 percent) went on to secondary prepara-

[1] The International Standard Classification of Education (ISCED) is a classification for organizing information on education and training by UNESCO. It is used for assembling, compiling, and presenting statistics both within countries and internationally (UNESCO, 2006). In the remainder of this report, we use this classification of educational levels for those readers who are most familiar with it as well as the terminology more commonly used in the KRI.

[2] We derived the number of students at each stage by following the basic-education graduating class of 2007 (that is, students who completed 9th grade that year) through subsequent years until 2011. The number of students progressing through each level of education may vary by cohort.

Figure 2.1
Progression of Students Through the TVET and Education System: Cohort that Graduated from Basic Education in 2007

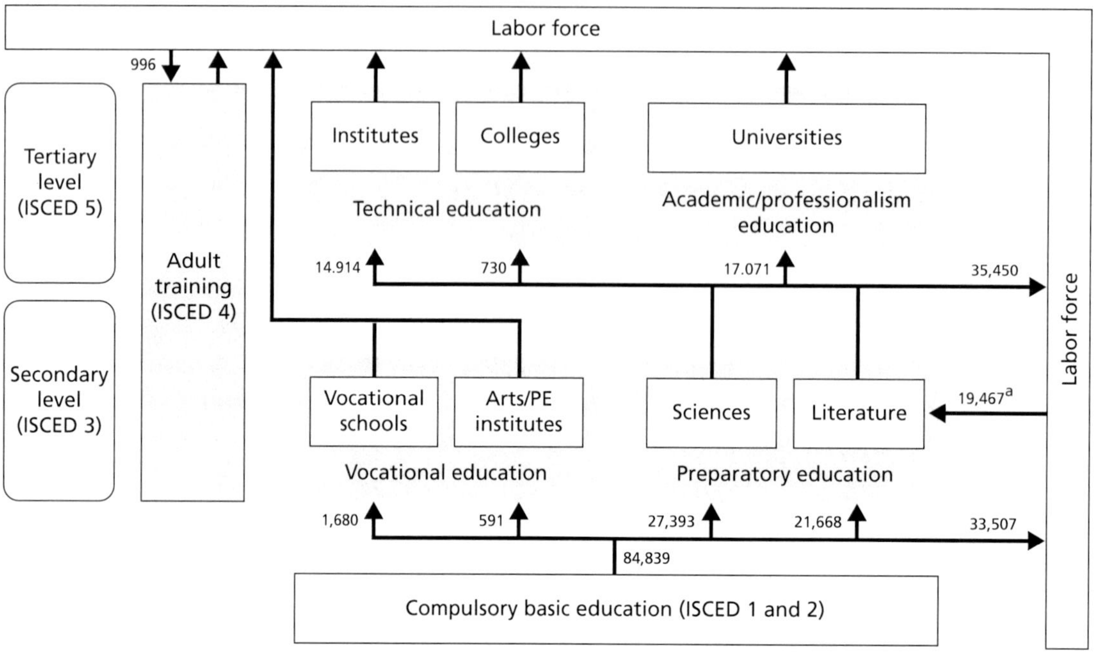

[a]These are individuals who had left schools and eventually returned to complete their secondary education.
SOURCES: MOE, MOHESR, and MOLSA.
RAND *RR277-2.1*

tory schools, 3 percent went on to vocational education and arts or physical education (PE) institutes, and the remainder (39 percent) left the education system. Of the students leaving the education system after completing basic education over the years, many later returned and completed their secondary education.

All students who attended secondary vocational education left the education system (with many entering the labor force) upon completing these programs of study.[3] Of the students who graduated from secondary education in 2010, more than half (52 percent) did not continue on with their studies, while 23 percent matriculated at a tertiary technical-education institute or college and the remaining 25 percent went on to academic or professional education at a university. Only about 1,000 adults completed training in an adult training center in 2010.

Altogether, these data indicate:

- The share of secondary students choosing vocational education (4 percent)[4] was low, while the share of post-secondary students assigned to tertiary technical education was relatively high (48 percent). The higher level of participation in tertiary technical education than in secondary vocational education is not common in other countries. In other devel-

---

3 Only the top two of each class may continue on to technical education provided they obtain the required score on the ministerial 12th grade exam. Few do so.

4 This percentage is for the 2007 cohort entering secondary education, and includes both those students entering vocational schools and arts/PE institutes.

oped and developing countries, the share of secondary school students participating in vocational education ranges from 30 to 70 percent, while that in tertiary technical education ranges from 20 to 40 percent (see Chapter Four).

- A sizable share of basic-education graduates (39 percent) and of secondary preparatory-education graduates (52 percent) did not continue their studies to the next level but instead left the education system and may have joined the labor force. Overall, some 70,000 students yearly may be joining the labor market without having received any specific preparation for employment.[5]
- There is no pathway for graduates from secondary vocational schools to continue on to tertiary education, either technical or academic.

Enrollment Trends

Over the past five years, enrollment trends have differed sharply between secondary vocational and tertiary technical education. Student enrollment in secondary vocational education diminished by half from 2006–07 to 2007–08, and although it increased slightly in subsequent years, it has not yet regained its previous higher level. By contrast, enrollment in technical institutes and colleges more than quadrupled between 2006–07 and 2010–11 (Figure 2.2).[6] In part to accommodate this growth, five new technical institutes have opened since 2006.

Due to the rapid growth of tertiary technical education, capacity in technical institutes is being stretched to the limit. Some institutes have begun to operate in two shifts, one from 8 a.m. to 2 p.m. and the second from 2 p.m. to 8 p.m. Morning classes are for recent graduates of secondary schools, while afternoon classes are for graduates of secondary schools who did not score high enough on the secondary ministerial exam for initial assignment to a technical college or who already have some working experience.

Interviewees explained that the divergence in enrollment trends between secondary vocational education and tertiary technical education might be due to a strong cultural bias against secondary vocational education. In addition, the vocational schools are older, have outdated curricula, and are less equipped than the technical institutes. Also, the institutes, like universities, appear to have received higher priority for physical and equipment upgrades in recent years. Thus, it is perhaps not surprising that secondary vocational education is a less attractive option for students and their families.

The adult training centers also have a limited capacity to serve a growing number of adults who do not continue past basic education or do not graduate from secondary education, along with older adults who want to upgrade or gain a new skill and possibly open a shop of their own.[7] In 2010–11, these centers served less than 1,000 adults. Demand for courses in technical centers may increase in the future due to the recent establishment of a Loan for

---

[5] The share of students completing basic education and moving on to secondary education has increased since education was mandated to grade 9 in 2008, and passing a 9th-grade exam was discontinued as a condition of continuing to secondary education. While 51,332 students entered secondary education in 2007, 82,309 did so in 2009, a 60 percent increase.

[6] Enrollment trends for non-tertiary training centers were not available.

[7] There may be unused capacity in existing training centers: In 2010–11, the Erbil's center offered 42 courses, but the Sulaimaniya's center offered only five courses and the Duhok's center only 12. The Erbil center decreased the length of its courses to offer them more frequently in order to accommodate demand.

Figure 2.2
Student Enrollment Trends in Secondary Vocational and Tertiary Technical Education, 2007–2012

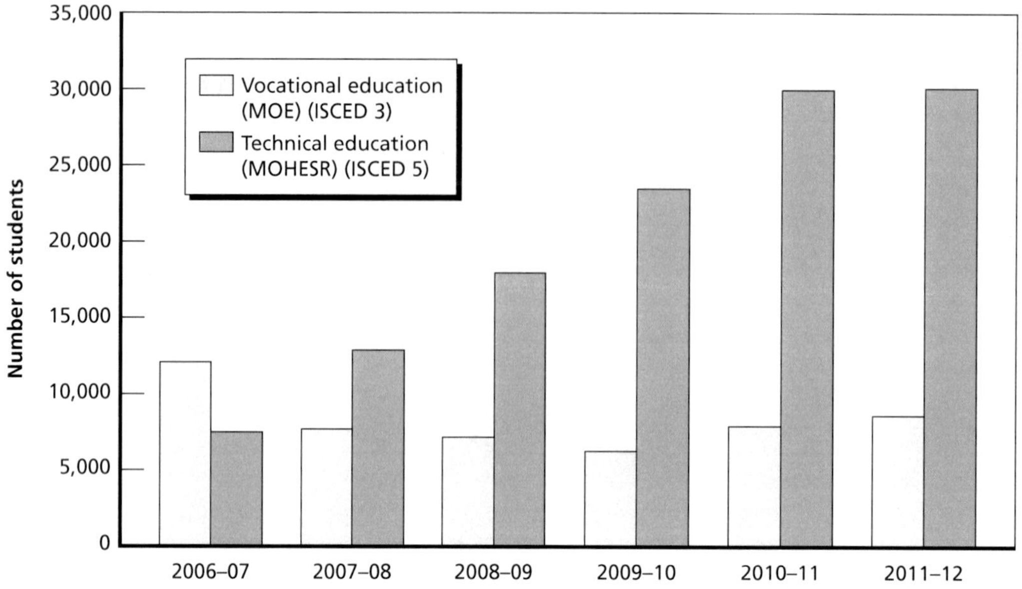

SOURCES: MOE and MOHESR.
RAND *RR277-2.2*

Small Projects program that provides up to 20 million Iraqi dinars (IQD) in six-year loans to individuals seeking to start a small business.

Participation by Gender

Females are as likely to participate in TVET as males. Females accounted for about half of all TVET students in 2011–12. Female participation in secondary vocational education has declined between 2007 and 2012 and is lower than female participation in adult training centers and in technical institutes where it increased between these two years (Figure 2.3).

Student Admission, Graduation Requirements, and Progression Opportunities

Admission Requirements and Assignment

At the secondary level, the choice of the vocational or the preparatory track is voluntary. As noted above, few students opt to pursue vocational education. In the past, students scoring less than 60 percent on the 9th-grade national exam were automatically assigned to vocational education. As a result, a larger number of students participated in this track in the past than at present.[8]

At the tertiary level, students who have completed secondary school must apply and score within a certain range on the 12th-grade KRG ministerial exam in order to be assigned by MOHESR to a university academic program or to technical education. Assignment to a spe-

8 The number of students in secondary vocational education peaked at 13,458 in 2005–06. In 2011–12, it was at 8,667.

Figure 2.3
Percentage of Female Participation in TVET, by Level of TVET, 2007 and 2012

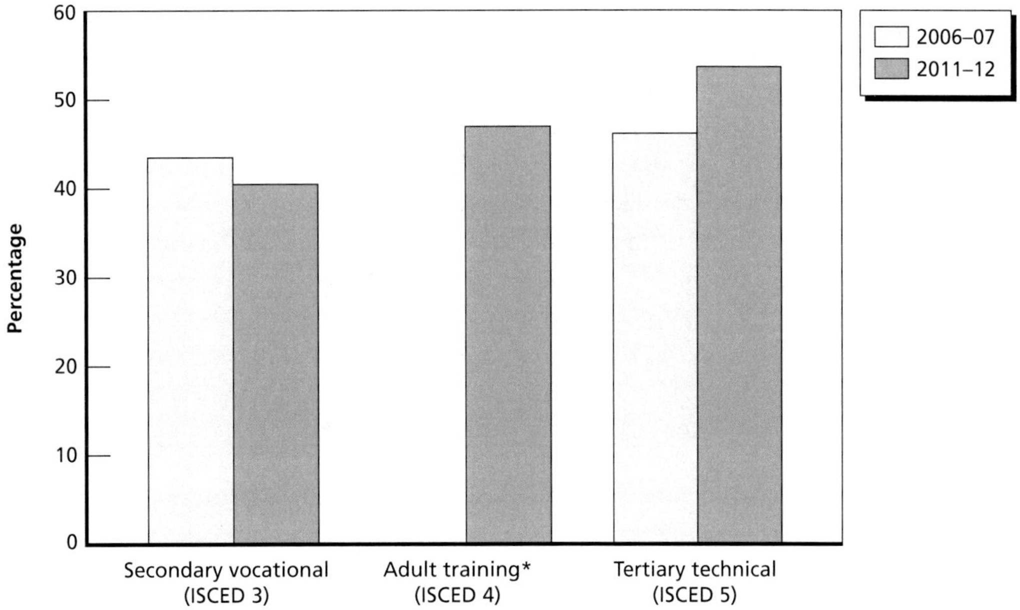

*Percentage for 2006-07 was not available.
SOURCES: MOE, MOLSA, and MOHESR.
RAND *RR277-2.3*

cific academic program or technical occupation is based on a student's preference and exam score, following a hierarchical scoring system. The hierarchy assigns the highest-scoring students to medical schools and then in descending scoring order to architecture, engineering, science, business, education, and technical education. Within technical education, there is a similar hierarchy of occupations, with health-related ones receiving the highest-eligible scoring students. Student preference is a determinant only if the student's score places them within the acceptable range for the subject area and institution of their preference. For instance, a student scoring 99 percent on the exam and who indicates a preference for medical studies in Erbil is likely to be assigned to that school because it is within the scoring range to be assigned to medical school. A student with the same preference scoring 80 percent will not be assigned to any medical school, but to a program that accepts students with that score or lower.[9]

For the 2011–12 academic year, 31,880 students applied for 28,325 places in university and technical education, with 3,505 of the lowest-scoring students (11 percent) on the final exam not admitted to either. For each institute and occupation offered within that institute, applicants are balanced against the number of available spaces, although the large number of eligible students may prompt MOHESR to assign more students than available capacity.

The MOLSA's training centers are open to all individuals aged 18 years or older who can read and write, including those who have not completed basic school. When demand for a training workshop exceeds available training places, applicants may be tested, interviewed,

[9] Under this practice, students have an incentive to indicate multiple preferences because the scoring threshold for each subject may vary from year to year. Students have only general knowledge of the expected score requirements based on previous years' experience.

and selected for participation by teachers. Participating students receive a 7,000 IQD stipend to cover general expenses (5,000 IQD) and transportation (2,000 IQD), presumably to encourage adults to upgrade their skills.

Graduation Requirements

All TVET students must pass a test to receive their certificate or diploma. At the end of the 12th grade, secondary vocational students take the same national ministerial exam as secondary preparatory students do, covering the same academic education subjects in addition to their occupational subject. Successful students receive a diploma.

At the tertiary level, there is no national assessment. Technical institute students take a final exam designed by each individual institute. This exam counts for 30 percent of the final score, while monthly/daily activities assessments account for the remaining 70 percent. The relative value placed on final exam and ongoing assessments was recently increased from 60 percent to encourage students to study continuously throughout the duration of their studies. Passing students receive a diploma from the institute.

The lack of a uniform national exam limits the value of this diploma as an indicator of competencies, which as a result may vary across institutes and across programs within institutes. In 2011, a uniform ministerial exam for all technical institutes was introduced and is expected to be implemented incrementally across all occupational subjects over the next five years.

MOLSA's training-center students are tested by their teachers and receive a certificate of participation.

Continuing Technical Education Opportunities

In 2011–12, students eligible for tertiary education were assigned about evenly between academic and technical education. Typically, few secondary-education vocational students take the ministerial exam and score high enough to pursue post-secondary studies, including technical education, limiting the attractiveness of the secondary vocational track in the KRI.

At the tertiary level, opportunities for technical institute students to continue from a two-year technical institute to a four-year college or university are also limited. Only the top two graduating students of each institute may go on to a four-year technical college or a university, provided that their final score is 80 percent or higher in all subjects.

Institutional Arrangements

Governance

Governance of the TVET system is split among three ministries, each of which coordinates with its counterpart in Baghdad (Figure 2.4). Offices under the supervision of a Director General oversee the MOE's secondary schools. Such offices also oversee MOLSA's adult training centers. Governance for MOHESR technical institutes and colleges is divided between two *Foundations of Technical Education*, one in Erbil that oversees the institutes and college in the governorates of Erbil and Duhok, and the other in Sulaimaniya that oversees the institutes and college in that governorate. Each foundation is quasi-autonomous and has a president who reports to the Minister of Higher Education and Scientific Research.

Figure 2.4
Governance of the KRI'S TVET System

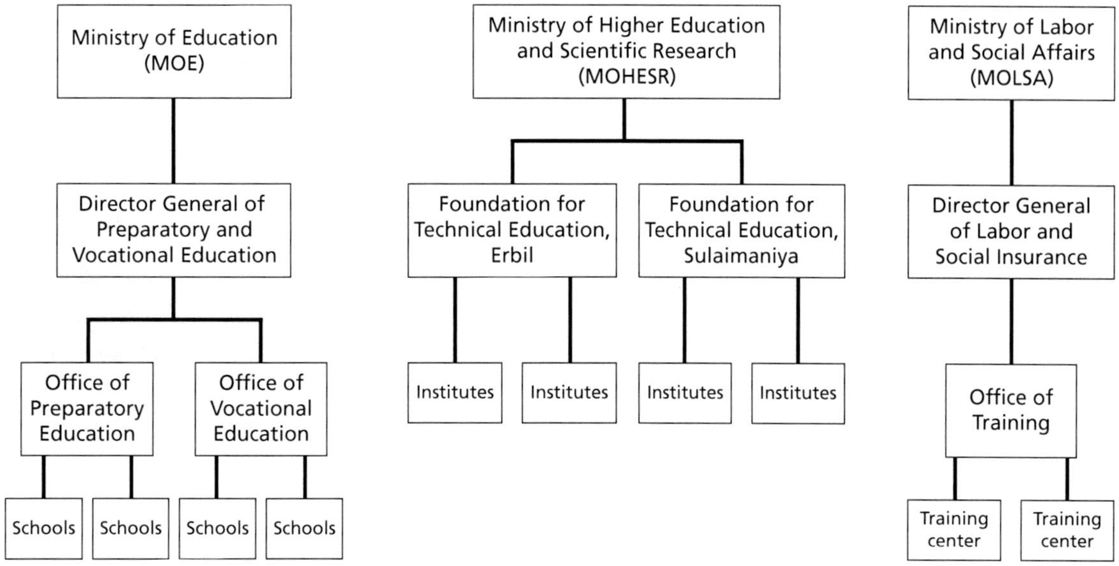

SOURCES: MOE, MOHESR, and MOLSA.
RAND *RR277-2.4*

Communications and collaboration between these different governing entities is not institutionalized but is reported to be informal.

Collaboration with the Private Sector

In contrast to most other countries, involvement of private-sector employers or trade unions in the governance, content, or management of TVET programs is not institutionalized in the KRI. Nevertheless, informal interactions with the private sector reportedly were increasing. For instance, the MOLSA's Erbil training center has contacted a local luxury hotel and a large carpentry firm for help in training the center's teachers. The MOHESR Foundations for Technical Education met with representatives of large firms to discuss why a newly opened mall had hired 600 foreigners for 700 positions. From this meeting, the MOHESR learned that the firms thought that institute graduates had insufficient command of English, inadequate computer skills, and needed more practical experience (a subject we will further discuss in the next chapter). A similar effort found that automobile firms thought institutes' students needed more training in electronics. A major obstacle TVET programs have faced in providing more relevant practical experience is inadequate equipment.

To date, none of the institutions responsible for overseeing TVET have attempted to anticipate or project economic and labor market needs. As a result, the mix of occupational training offered and the number of students enrolled in each occupation offered may have little relationship with the needs of the labor market. Similarly, failure to gather information on the employers' skills requirements may lead to the development of skills that differ from or are inadequate to meet those in demand.

Financing

The government entirely finances TVET programs in the KRI. Contributions from employers or students are not mandated, although students in the afternoon training sessions of technical institutes, many of whom have some working experience, pay the equivalent of 300 to 400 U.S. dollars per year. International governments and NGOs have donated some equipment, buildings, and training.

Curriculum

The current curricula of the three types of TVET programs vary in duration and balance between general education and occupational training. Table 2.1 summarizes curriculum characteristics for vocational schools, tertiary technical institutes and colleges, and training centers. The secondary vocational curriculum lasts three years, while tertiary technical education is mostly two years.[10] The duration of training in MOLSA training centers is shorter, depending on the center and the occupation.

Time spent on general-education subjects (mathematics, languages, and religion) varies across vocational schools by the type of occupational training. In technical institutes, the whole curriculum is oriented toward occupations, with about 40 percent theory and 60 percent in classroom practice, except for business administration, for which theory dominates.

None of the TVET programs offer structured on-the-job training experience. Hands-on practical training is limited to a two-month internship in the private or government sector during the summer break. Students are given an introduction letter but must find their own internship placement. Supervision of internships is minimal, and employers only certify attendance.

Table 2.1
Curriculum Characteristics, by Type of TVET Program

Curriculum Characteristic	Secondary Vocational (ISCED 3)	Tertiary Technical (ISCED 5)	Adult Training (ISCED 4)
Duration (years)	3	2	.2 to .5
Percentage of time spent on occupational training	37–60[a]	100	100
Duration of practical internship (months)	2	2	None
Language of teaching	Kurdish	English[b]	Kurdish

SOURCES: MOE, MOHESR, and MOLSA.

[a] In secondary vocational, the percentage of time spent on occupational training varies. It is 37 percent of the total school time for trade, 52 percent for commercial, and 60 percent for agricultural occupations.

[b] In practice, however, much of the teaching is done in Kurdish because of lack of English proficiency among both teachers and students.

---

[10] Two four-year technical colleges recently were established. They reportedly place greater emphasis on practical classroom experience than engineering colleges in universities.

Teaching in the vocational schools and technical centers is in Kurdish. Although teaching in the technical institutes and colleges is supposed to be in English, it is not always so due to the lack of English proficiency of most students and teachers.

The need to modernize the curricula in all TVET programs is acute. Most curricula are reportedly 10 to 20 years old, if not older. Staff at all three ministries said they are planning to revise their curricula. To this end, the MOE has formed a committee and a Directorate of Curriculum has been established in each of the two Foundations for Technical Education. MOLSA is planning to review its curricula with assistance from the International Labour Organization (ILO).

Ideally, the secondary vocational-education and tertiary technical-education curricula should be aligned so that students can advance from lower to higher levels and have the opportunity to gain increasingly complex knowledge and skills in the same occupational area. Yet our respondents indicated that no efforts were being made to align curricula in a way that would create a coordinated pathway from secondary vocational to tertiary technical studies. This is a major issue, because it provides a strong disincentive for graduates of basic education to choose secondary vocational education instead of preparatory academic education. Also, the result is a level of tertiary technical education in the KRI that more closely resembles the level of secondary vocational education than the more specialized and higher skilled technical level typically taught at the tertiary level.

Occupational Training Programs

Vocational schools and technical centers offer ten and seven programs, respectively, in the trade occupations, including automotive, carpentry, computers, and electricity. In 2010–11, these occupations accounted for about half of enrollment in vocational schools. Commerce accounted for one-third, and agriculture, with four programs, accounted for one-tenth. In adult technical centers, trade occupations accounted for two-thirds of enrollment (Table 2.2). Both vocational schools and training centers only recently added programs in the use of information and computer technology (IT).

Not all individual vocational schools and training centers offer training in all occupations. About one-third of the 32 vocational schools specialize in commerce, while another third specialize in trade occupations. The remaining schools offer a mix of occupational offerings, but typically not all of them.

The technical institutes offer a broader range of occupational offerings, covering 50 specialties in the trade accounting/administration, agricultural, IT, medical, media, and tourism fields (Table 2.2). The accounting/administration occupations accounted for more than half of enrollment, presumably because they are the type of occupations that best prepares students for government jobs. As noted later in this chapter, secondary as well as tertiary education graduates have a strong preference to work for the government, which currently employ more than 50 percent of the active labor force. About 15 percent of enrollment was in medical-related occupations, including nursing. Another 12 percent was in trade occupations, with electricity and surveying having the highest enrollment.[11]

[11] Tables A.1 and A.2 in Appendix A provide a complete list of occupational programs offered at each level of TVET.

Table 2.2
Number of Occupational Programs and Number and Percentage of Students, by Occupational Group and TVET Level, 2011–2012

	Secondary Vocational (ISCED 3)			Adult Training (ISCED 4)			Tertiary Technical (ISCED 5)		
Occupational Group	Number of Programs	Number of Students	Percentage of Students	Number of Programs	Number of Students	Percentage of Students	Number of Programs	Number of Students	Percentage of Students
Trade/ technical	10	4,101	52.7	7	955	95.9	13	3,672	12.2
Accounting/ administra-tion	1	2,856	36.7	—	—	—	9	15,705	52.3
Agriculture	4	822	10.5	—	—	—	9	1,480	4.9
IT	—	—	—	—	—	—	1	2,630	8.8
Medical	—	—	—	—	—	—	10	4,396	14.6
Other	—	—	—	2	41	4.1	8	2,149	7.2
Total	15	7,779	100.0	9	996	100.0	50	30,038	100.0

SOURCES: Tables A.1 and A.2 in Appendix A.

NOTES: Data for secondary vocational and adult training are for 2010–11, and data for tertiary technical are for 2011–12; a dash means there are no occupational programs for this occupational group.

Like vocational schools and training centers, an individual institute offers only a subset of these occupational offerings, with some as few as three and others with as many as 25 occupations. Two institutes specialize in administration (Erbil and Duhok), two in agriculture (Erbil and Sulaimaniya), one in medicine and health (Erbil), and one in computer science (Sulaimaniya). The other 17 technical institutes provide training for varying combinations of the 50 occupational areas.

In the absence of data on occupational trends in the KRI's economy, it is not possible to assess whether the growth in the supply of graduates trained in the various occupations is consistent with demand. As noted above, there is no formal relationship or collaboration between the three TVET programs and the private sector to help determine and adjust the supply of occupational offerings to demand. In addition, interviewees at vocational schools and technical institutes estimated that only about 20 percent of their graduates found jobs within two years in their trained fields. This is not to say that the mix of occupational offerings has remained constant. Through informal exchanges among TVET providers, several new occupational offerings have been added in recent years. These have included sewing and tourism in some training centers, tailoring and fashion design in some vocational schools, and IT-related training in both. Some technical institutes have added offerings in agricultural guidance, IT, marketing, civil engineering, transport, oil, and tourism. Enrollment in these new programs was still small in 2012, varying from 69 in marketing to 159 in oil, 207 in civil engineering, and 327 in tourism guidance.

Teacher Recruitment, Qualifications, and Training

Teacher Recruitment and Assignment

The Ministry of Education recruits and assigns teachers for vocational schools. By contrast, at the tertiary level, recruitment is decentralized within each institute and within individual departments. Permanent departmental hires must be approved by the respective institutes, the relevant Foundation for Technical Education, and the MOHESR. Non-permanent teachers, hired on a contract basis, need only be approved at the institute level.

Teacher Qualifications

Secondary vocational education teachers now must have a bachelor's degree in an appropriate specialty. Teachers of tertiary technical education must have a master's or doctoral degree. Rapid enrollment growth in technical education, however, means that technical institutes mostly have hired teachers with a bachelor's degree and on a contract basis. In Sulaimaniya, the Foundation for Technical Education reported having 200 permanent teachers with master's or doctoral degrees, but it had 500 teachers on contract. The current shortage of teachers with a master's or doctoral degree may be alleviated over the coming years as the number of such graduates increases.

TVET teachers at any level are not required to have practical experience in the occupational specialty they teach. Practical experience was once required at the tertiary level, but is no longer required, presumably because of recruitment difficulties. Nevertheless, some teachers in vocational schools and technical institutes may have had practical experience through owning their own business or working in the private sector. Reportedly, this is particularly the case for teachers in the health, electricity, electronics, mechanics, and media departments.

In-Service Teacher Training

No formal continuing in-service training is required and provided to TVET teachers at any level. The only training provided for permanent teachers is initial training in teaching methods. For secondary vocational teachers, this training occurs on the job under the supervision of a more experienced teacher. Permanent teachers at the tertiary technical institutes and colleges are required to participate in 90 hours of formal training in teaching methods, but contract teachers are not required to do so.

Recently, UNESCO and the British Council instituted several programs to train TVET teachers. About 40 principals and supervisors of vocational schools participated in workshops in Germany and other countries. A limited number of vocational-education teachers (two to three per department) participated in training workshops focused on curriculum development. Similarly, a limited number of selected technical-education teachers participated in "training-the-trainers" workshops. Also, management courses were provided to the heads of tertiary technical education departments.

TVET teachers are eligible to participate in the KRG's extensive capacity-development program, which sends KRG employees abroad to obtain a post-secondary degree. Since 2010–11, the MOHESR has required that teachers of technical education accumulate 50 to 100 hours of development-credit hours annually through active participation in conferences, seminars, academic workshops, research, or publication. These teachers must also present a seminar every six months and prepare presentations on an international scientific article every six months (MOHESR, 2010).

Teaching Equipment

The quality and relevance of the TVET training that students receive depends in large part on whether the theories and equipment used in the training are up to date. Generally, our respondents said that one of their biggest problems was insufficient and aging equipment, an assessment that our visits to a few institutes and vocational schools confirmed.

Post-Graduation Employment Opportunities

TVET programs provide no job placement or referral services to their graduates. TVET graduates, like graduates from secondary and tertiary institutions, have a strong preference to work for the government, which currently employs 50 percent of workers in the KRI (KRLFS, 2012). Unlike the evolving private sector, government employment provides more flexible and shorter working hours as well as generous vacation and other benefits, including a lifelong pension. Government employment also provides the flexibility to take a second, private-sector job. Our respondents consistently said that private employment, if a choice at all, was a second choice for most.

Nevertheless, the large number of graduates from all levels of education entering the labor market every year, and the desire of the KRG government to encourage private-sector growth, are likely to ensure that most graduates will eventually have to look to the private sector for employment. As it is, our respondents noted that TVET graduates have difficulties finding public- or private-sector employment and that only 10 to 20 percent of TVET graduates find work within six months of graduation.[12]

One potential reason for the difficulty that graduates from TVET face in finding private employment is the higher number of graduates than the current economy is able to absorb, especially from tertiary education. Enrollment and graduation trends reviewed earlier show that the number of graduates has more than quadrupled in the past five years. It also may be due to a mismatch between the number of students trained in each occupation and the number that KRI's employers need. As noted earlier, the main determinants of enrollment in TVET occupations are provider capacity, student preference, and exam score. As a result, the number of students assigned to various occupations is institutionally determined rather than employer demand-driven. Another potential reason that graduates have difficulties finding private-sector jobs may be an "employability" or "soft-skill" gap. We discuss issues of matching supply with demand in the next chapter.

Ongoing and Planned TVET Improvement Initiatives

All three ministries overseeing components of the KRI's TVET system have initiatives under way or plan to enhance their programs. Several international organizations also are helping improve TVET in Iraq, including in the KRI.

---

[12] As noted in Chapter One, youth (aged 15 to 24) unemployment is relatively high at 18 percent, and labor force participation low at 20 percent (KRLFS, 2012).

Ministry of Education

The MOE is building three new large secondary vocational-education centers, one in each capital of the three governorates. Each will serve 6,000 to 10,000 students, more than tripling the capacity of the current MOE vocational schools. The vocational schools located in the governorates' capitals will be integrated with these new centers, while the current regional vocational schools will remain open. Each center will have dormitories for students. The MOE is further considering a goal of having 20 percent of basic-education graduates continue in vocational education, which would be a more than five-fold increase in the proportion currently doing so. The MOE further anticipates that 25 percent of the graduates from vocational schools eventually will continue occupational education in MOHESR's technical institutes.

These new vocational-education centers are expected to open as early as 2014. They initially will offer the same agricultural, commercial, and trade-occupational programs as the current vocational schools. Over time, the current commercial offering will be divided into three programs: administration, accounting, and science of computers and banks. Planned additional trade-related programs include cooling and air conditioning, telecommunication, electrical elevators, maintenance of medical equipment, and printing. The centers plan to eventually offer programs of study in 21 occupations (currently 14)—which may still be too few, given their planned enrollment size.

Ministry of Higher Education and Scientific Research

MOHESR may build a teaching hospital to train students. It also plans to include a training program for the oil industry in three institutes. Currently, few training opportunities are offered in occupations related to the oil industry, a sector for priority development in the KRI.

MOHESR, as part of its reform effort, is planning to decentralize its governance and is making changes to its form of technical education. The two Foundations for Technical Education will be converted into three polytechnic universities, one in the capital of each governorate. The distinction between the two-year institutes and four-year colleges will be maintained, but all students would first start in two-year institutes, graduating with a diploma. The top 25 percent of graduating students would continue to four-year colleges, graduating with a bachelor's degree. The current two-month internship will be replaced by six months of on-the-job training. Those students continuing to four-year colleges would do an additional six months on-the job training (MOHESR, 2010).

Ministry of Labor and Social Affairs

MOLSA is opening two additional technical centers—one in Garmyan district and one in Soran. It has signed a memorandum of understanding (MOU) with Scania, a Swedish company, to train 30 to 40 mechanics to specialize in repairs of trucks and heavy-duty equipment.[13] Applicants ranging in age from 16 to 30 years old and with some work experience are eligible to participate.

---

[13] Iraq is the 14th largest market for Scania's products, and is projected to eventually become the 10th largest.

Other Initiatives

British Council

With European Union funding, the British Council is implementing a three-part effort to develop TVET Iraq-wide, including in the KRI. The first part involves developing a TVET strategy for all of Iraq. To this end, stakeholders, including representatives of the MOE, MOHESR, MOLSA, and the private sector, are being convened for strategy sessions.

Second, the British Council is developing standards for selected occupations. It has identified five priority areas—oil and gas, car maintenance, air conditioning, bakery operation, and travel services—through private sector and TVET staff interviews and is developing curricula for each of these areas.

Third, to test the new standards and curricula, the British Council plans to establish five vocational centers of excellence. Two of these reportedly will be in the KRI; one will focus on tourism and the other on either air conditioning or car maintenance. School leaders and teachers will be trained on the standards and curricula, and the centers of excellence were said to begin operation in late 2012.

UNESCO

With the involvement of a Steering Committee that includes MOLSA, the MOE, Foundations for Technical Education, and the Chamber of Commerce, UNESCO is contracting a project to design and implement two pilot initiatives of private-sector partnerships with TVET providers. The contractor is expected to develop template agreements defining duties and responsibilities of the parties, including on-the-job training, field visits, collaboration in curriculum design, and feedback on skills needed. The contractor also will recommend incentives that the government can put in place to increase private-sector willingness to participate and to increase a sense of corporate social responsibility.

UNESCO also is planning to develop a manual on skills required for employability and entrepreneurship. It will cover communication, school-to-work transition, entrepreneurial skills, as well as how to write a curriculum vitae, deal with others, and deal with conflict at work.

UNESCO also plans to train 24 vocational teachers in modern teaching methods to serve as a model training program. The training will include an Internet distance-learning component as well as a face-to-face component.

Summary

Improving the access, relevance, and quality of TVET are objectives of the KRG, which is taking steps in recent years to achieve this objective. Enrollment in tertiary technical education has increased more rapidly than that for any other type of education at the secondary or tertiary levels. Today, about 50 percent of tertiary students graduate with a technical diploma, up from 27 percent in 2007. While the KRI has made progress toward expanding access and providing equal opportunity for males and females to enroll in TVET, a number of challenges remain.

The focus placed on tertiary technical education has been accompanied by the neglect of secondary vocational education, for which enrollment has been low and stagnant in recent years. A large number of secondary-school graduates who do not continue to tertiary education may not be adequately prepared to join the labor force. Similarly, technical training remains extremely limited for adults who drop out of basic or secondary education or who may want to upgrade their skills. However, the planned MOE large secondary vocational education centers in each governorate may triple access of secondary students to vocational education in the near future. Similarly, MOLSA has plans to build additional centers. It also is partnering with a private company to provide tailored technical training opportunities. This approach, if successful, may be worth emulating more broadly in the future.

Perhaps one of the most important remaining challenges will be developing an institutionalized relationship between TVET providers and the private sector. This partnership will be important for:

- matching the type of and enrollment in TVET occupational training to the evolving occupational demand of the economy
- upgrading occupational standards and the curricula to incorporate the skills desired by employers
- increasing the opportunities for on-the-job training.

Currently, student assignment to TVET occupations depends more on institutional supply than on labor-market demand. The number and mix of occupational programs has remained mostly unchanged over time and insufficiently diverse, especially in secondary vocational schools and MOLSA's training centers. Although TVET curricula specify a two-month internship in the government or private sector, it is not necessarily related to the students' area of studies and lacks quality assurance. Nevertheless, one reform planned for tertiary TVET is to increase on-the-job training to six months in the two-year programs and one year for the four-year programs. This makes it even more crucial to start developing partnerships with employers.

Another challenge is the low quality of TVET education, which often has obsolete curricula. UNESCO and other organizations, including TVET-provider curriculum-development committees, are beginning to address this through occasional and short-duration train-the-trainer curriculum-development programs. Still, much remains to be done on a continuing basis to increase and institutionalize the local capacity to revise and develop curricula. New curricula also will require upgrading the preparation of thousands of teachers. In the past, teachers have not had the opportunity to keep up with developments in their occupational field. Teachers may need retraining as workshop equipment is modernized. In addition, curricula for the academic subjects in the secondary vocational programs have not experienced the same updates and reforms that the curricula of the secondary preparatory programs have. Therefore, students who wish to progress from secondary to tertiary TVET typically lack the academic skills to do so.

TVET governance also needs attention. It is currently divided among three ministries with separate and centralized policy and operational control. There is little coordination across the ministries responsible for TVET, so the curricula are not aligned among the different levels. Centralization of decisions about occupational offerings, curriculum design, and student qualification standards also may limit the ability of TVET providers to respond to local market demands.

Most students and families perceive TVET to be second to academic education. At both the secondary and tertiary levels, lower-performing students choose or are assigned to TVET.

Given the growing importance of TVET in preparing students for work in the developing economy, there is little reason to limit access or to discourage enrollment of high-performing students in TVET. The system will need to significantly improve in quality and outcomes to attract better students, however.

A final challenge is to provide reliable and consistent signals to employers about the qualifications of TVET graduates. With the exception of secondary vocational education, which has a uniform national graduation exam, certification of the "competence" of tertiary technical-education graduating students is left to individual teachers, institutions, or centers. Consequently, there is no standard by which employers can judge whether graduates are adequately prepared for employment.

CHAPTER THREE

Labor and Skill Needs in the KRI Economy

Education and training institutions require systematic information about the demand for employees and skills in order to set occupational standards, to determine what occupational programs to offer, to determine the level of student enrollment desirable, and to design curricula. Data on the skills requirements of the private sector in particular have not been collected, yet are essential to promoting its further growth and development.

This chapter relies primarily on data from the 2012 Kurdistan Region Labor Force Survey[1] and the RAND Survey of Business Establishments also fielded in 2012 to analyze current employment patterns in the KRI to gain a full picture of where jobs are concentrated and how that matches up to the supply of secondary versus postsecondary TVET graduates; assess the work-readiness of the local labor force as perceived by employers, to identify the skills gaps that need to be addressed; and assess employer demands for skills to inform our recommendations for improving the alignment of TVET provision with labor market needs.

Our analysis revealed a number of important findings. Currently, the government employs about half of the labor force. We find that a secondary vocational education may provide adequate preparation for more than two-thirds of jobs in the KRI economy. A significant share of employers rate the preparation of graduates as poor—more than one-third of employers say that graduates from secondary and tertiary KRI education institutions are not ready for work. Employers who face difficulties finding candidates for jobs have the most difficulties hiring for technical, sales and customer service, process plant, and machine operator occupations. Employers indicated that graduates from KRI education institutions need writing and numeracy, IT, and hands-on technical skills, as well as to a lesser extent language skills. Surveyed employers emphasized "soft" skills, including oral and communication skills and the ability to interact and communicate with customers, and our interviews with select employers revealed that these were in short supply in the KRI.

In interpreting the results of our survey of employers, readers should keep in mind two limitations. First, our survey covered only the more formal segment of the private-sector KRI economy. Small firms with fewer than five employees were not included in our survey. It may be that employers in this segment of the economy may be less demanding of skills than the employers we surveyed. However, they are likely to equally benefit from an upgraded preparation of entrants to the labor force. Second, employer responses to the survey questions reflect their perception of the skills their employees possess and of the skills they need, rather than an actual measure of the performance of their employees or the skills that jobs require.

---

[1] The design and fielding of this survey was a collaborative effort of RAND and the Kurdistan Region Statistics Office (KRSO) undertaken in the context of another related RAND study. For details, see Abramzon et al. (2013).

Current Employment Patterns in the KRI

Currently, the KRI's main employment sectors are:

- government, consisting of the ministries (e.g., Health, Education, Electricity) and other exclusively government institutions responsible for the delivery of public services (51 percent)
- construction (13 percent)
- wholesale and retail trade (11 percent)
- agriculture, hunting, and fishing (6 percent)
- transportation (6 percent).

Table 3.1 ranks specific economic activities by the proportion of employees within them, separating government and private activities. Public administration and defense together comprise the largest share of employment in the KRI, at 23 percent. Education accounts for the second-largest share of employment in government and the fourth-largest overall. Within the private sector, construction accounts for the largest share of employment and the second largest overall, while wholesale and retail trades account for the second-largest share of private employment and the third-largest overall. Six percent of all KRI employees work in the agricultural sector.

There are no formal economic growth forecasts available for the KRI. The KRG is, however, seeking to increase the private sector's share of total employment. Within the private sector, growth may occur in wholesale and retail trade, transportation, and financial and real estate services in part due to the increased oil exploitation activity in the region. Also, retrospective research on economic trends suggests that growth in KRI-comparison countries[2] typically has occurred in "non-tradable" sectors such as services (retail, hotel, and tourism), wholesale trade, and transportation (Shatz et al., 2012).[3] Construction also is expected to continue to be a major source of employment. At the same time, the KRI may face difficulties developing a competitive manufacturing sector given the comparative advantage of other countries in the region. Retrospective research further suggests that manufacturing has not been a major source of employment growth in comparison countries (Shatz et al., 2012).

TVET Could Prepare Individuals for Most Jobs

Table 3.2 shows current total and private sector employment in the KRI grouped into three main occupational categories:

---

[2] Comparison countries included Argentina, Azerbaijan, Colombia, Ecuador, Kazakhstan, Malaysia, Romania, Peru, South Africa, and Venezuela, covering their respective economic growth from 1995 to 2008. Most of these countries are rich in energy or natural resources, as is the KRI.

[3] Non-tradable goods are those that are consumed where produced. They include construction and services (accommodations, personal services, tourism). Tradable goods are generally sold on the international market. They include agricultural goods, mined metals, and oil.

Table 3.1
Percentage of Employees, by Sector, 2012

Sector	All Employees
Government	
Public administration and military	23
Education	10
Police and security	4
Administrative and support services	3
Human health and social work	3
Utilities (electricity, water, and waste)	2
Other[a]	6
Subtotal	51
Private	
Construction	13
Wholesale and retail trade	11
Agriculture, hunting, and fishing	6
Transportation and storage	6
Other personal and social services	4
Professional, scientific, and technical	2
Manufacturing	1
Accommodations and food services	1
Real estate	1
Household production	1
Other[b]	4
Subtotal	50
Total	100

SOURCE: KRLFS (2012).

NOTE: Government sector includes government and state-owned enterprises. Private sector includes private, mixed, Kurdish or Iraq NGO, foreign private, foreign government or nongovernmental organization (NGO). Total may not add up to 100 percent because of rounding.

[a] Includes economic activities dominated by the government sector but also have modest private sector involvement.

[b] Includes economic activities dominated by the private sector but also have modest government sector involvement. Also includes sectors with a very small share of employment such as mining and quarrying (0.2 percent), information and communication (0.3), finance and insurance (0.1), arts entertainment and recreation (0.2), and activities of extraterritorial bodies (0.2).

Table 3.2
Percentage of All and Private Sector Employees, by Occupation, 2012

Occupation	All Employees	Private Sector Employees
Occupations requiring tertiary education		
Managers	4	3
Professionals	11	5
Technicians and associate professionals	3	2
Subtotal	18	10
Occupations for which secondary vocational education preparation may provide sufficient preparation		
Clerical support workers	14	2
Service and sales workers	23	34
Skilled agricultural, forestry, and fishery workers	6	11
Craft and related trades workers	9	18
Plant and machine operators and assemblers	5	8
Subtotal	56	72
Elementary occupations	12	18
Armed forces occupations	14	1
Total	100	100

SOURCE: KRLFS (2012).
NOTE: Totals may not add to 100 due to rounding.

- occupations that typically require tertiary academic or technical education
- occupations for which secondary vocational education may provide sufficient preparation
- occupations that typically require no particular preparation, or "elementary occupations."[4]

The resulting pattern of employment by occupation suggests that most jobs in the KRI economy may require no more than secondary vocational training. Most employees (72 percent) in the private sector are in occupations for which secondary vocational education may be sufficient, such as service workers, trades and crafts workers, and plant and machine operators. Professionals, as well as technicians and associate professionals who typically must obtain a tertiary education, are disproportionately employed in the government sector. They account for a relatively small 18 percent of all employees, and only 10 percent of private sector employees.

Just as it is for the overall KRI economy, the majority of jobs in nearly all sectors of the economy are in occupations for which a secondary vocational education may be sufficient. For instance, in the manufacturing sector, 72 percent of employees are in such occupations, while 13 percent are in occupations that require a tertiary education and 15 percent are in occupations that require no formal education (Table 3.3). For the wholesale and retail trade sector, a higher level—87 percent—of employees are in occupations for which secondary vocational

[4] Appendix B provides a more detailed occupational classification.

Table 3.3
Percentage of Private-Sector Employees, by Type of Occupation and Sector, 2012

Sector	Occupations Requiring Tertiary Education (ISCED 5)	Occupations for Which Secondary Vocational Education May Be Sufficient (ISCED 3)	Occupations Requiring No Formal Education	Total
Agriculture, hunting, and fishing	4	93	4	100
Manufacturing	13	72	15	100
Construction	9	64	27	100
Wholesale and retail trade	6	87	8	100
Transportation and storage	6	73	22	100
Accommodations and food services	9	44	47	100
Real estate	16	72	12	100
Professional, scientific, and technical	26	60	14	100
Other personal and social services	8	61	31	100
Household production	3	89	8	100
Other	26	52	23	100
All private employees	9	72	18	100
All employees	21	66	13	100

SOURCE: KRLFS (2012).

NOTE: Totals may not add to 100 due to rounding.

education may be sufficient, but only 6 percent are in occupations requiring a tertiary education, and another 8 percent are in occupations requiring no formal education. In other sectors, the share of employees in occupations for which secondary vocational education may be sufficient ranges from 52 to 93 percent.

In sum, current employment patterns indicate that secondary vocational education could play a significant role in training future labor-market entrants. Most jobs in the private sector rely on individuals with vocational skills. Vocational education programs could support initial preparation for those jobs.

Employers' Hiring Experiences

While individuals without a tertiary education could perform most jobs within the KRI, employers indicate that the individuals they hire are not always well prepared for work. Some occupations have been particularly difficult to fill, leading employers to search outside the KRI. Below, we review what KRI employers told us about the work-readiness of local graduates from secondary and tertiary educational institutions, occupations that are particularly difficult to fill, and how they sometimes turn outside the KRI to fill their workforce needs.

Work-Readiness of Local Labor

A significant share of employers we surveyed said that graduates from local education and TVET institutions were not well prepared for work. About 40 percent of employers said that graduates from secondary schools were poorly or very poorly prepared for work, and a smaller share (25 percent) said that graduates from tertiary institutions—both technical institutes and universities—are poorly or very poorly prepared for work (Figure 3.1). Also, 25 percent of employers said they had difficulties filling positions that required a secondary education. The most common shortcomings they encountered include:

- lack of prior work experience, cited by 40 percent of employers
- lack of educational qualifications for the job (31 percent)
- lack of appropriate skills (21 percent).

Other studies have reported similar findings. Fifty-one percent of private firms surveyed in Sulaimaniya and 32 percent of firms surveyed in Erbil said that an inadequately educated workforce was a major constraint to their business (World Bank, 2012). And a survey of mainly small and medium-sized enterprises (i.e., enterprises with three to 30 employees) across 15 governorates in Iraq found that in Erbil governorate, employers' main concerns with their employees were a lack of appropriate skills for the required tasks and a lack of workplace discipline (USAID-Iraq, 2010). Finally, about 78 percent of car maintenance and 40 percent or more of telecommunications firms surveyed by UNESCO and ICON Institute (2012) said that both

Figure 3.1
Percentage of Employers, by How Well Prepared for Work Local Graduates Are and Level of Education, 2012

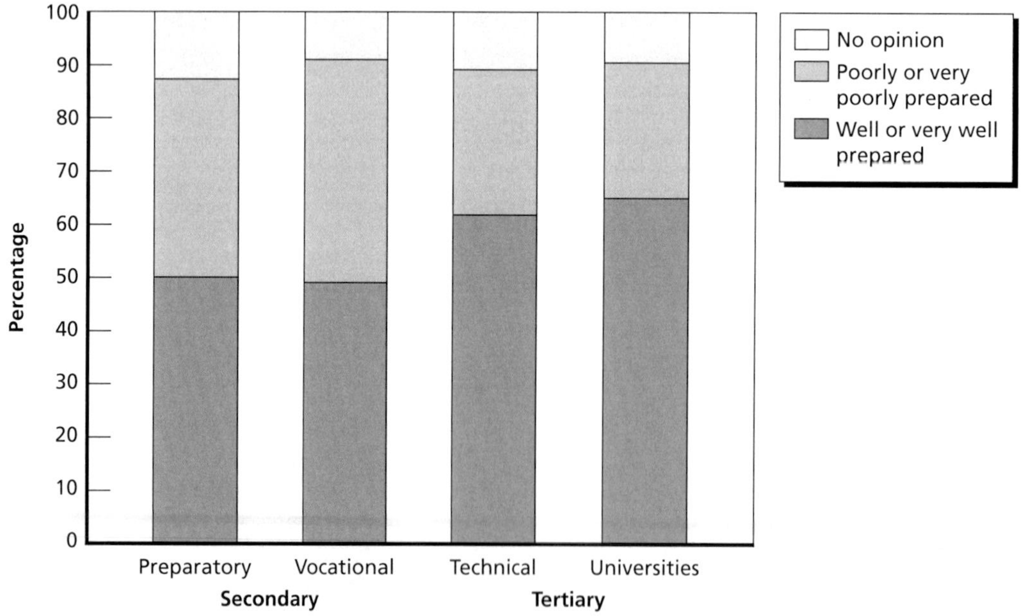

SOURCE: RAND Survey of Business Establishments (2012).
NOTE: N = 360. The survey question was, "How prepared for work are graduates from <type of school> within the Kurdistan Region of Iraq?"
RAND *RR277-3.1*

graduates from secondary schools and from tertiary technical institutes were poorly or very poorly prepared for work.

Most Difficult Occupations to Hire from Within the KRI

Overall, close to 30 percent of employers surveyed reported having difficulties hiring within the KRI for certain types of occupations. Employers most frequently mentioned technical occupations (37 percent) as being difficult to hire for locally (Figure 3.2). About 20 percent of employers had difficulties hiring across a range of other occupations, including sales and customer service, personal services, process plant and machine operators, and trades.

Employers Meet Some Workforce Needs Outside of the KRI

Another indicator that the local labor force is not adequately prepared to meet private-sector employers' needs is the large share of employers (50 percent) that reported hiring employees from outside the KRI. The average share of employees from elsewhere across surveyed employers was 17 percent (Figure 3.3).[5] Larger employers were significantly more likely to have employees from outside the KRI than both small and medium-sized employers, while the average shares of employees not from the KRI in both mining and manufacturing and infra-

Figure 3.2
Percentage of Employers Who Have Difficulties Hiring Local Labor, by Type of Occupation They Have Difficulty Hiring, 2012

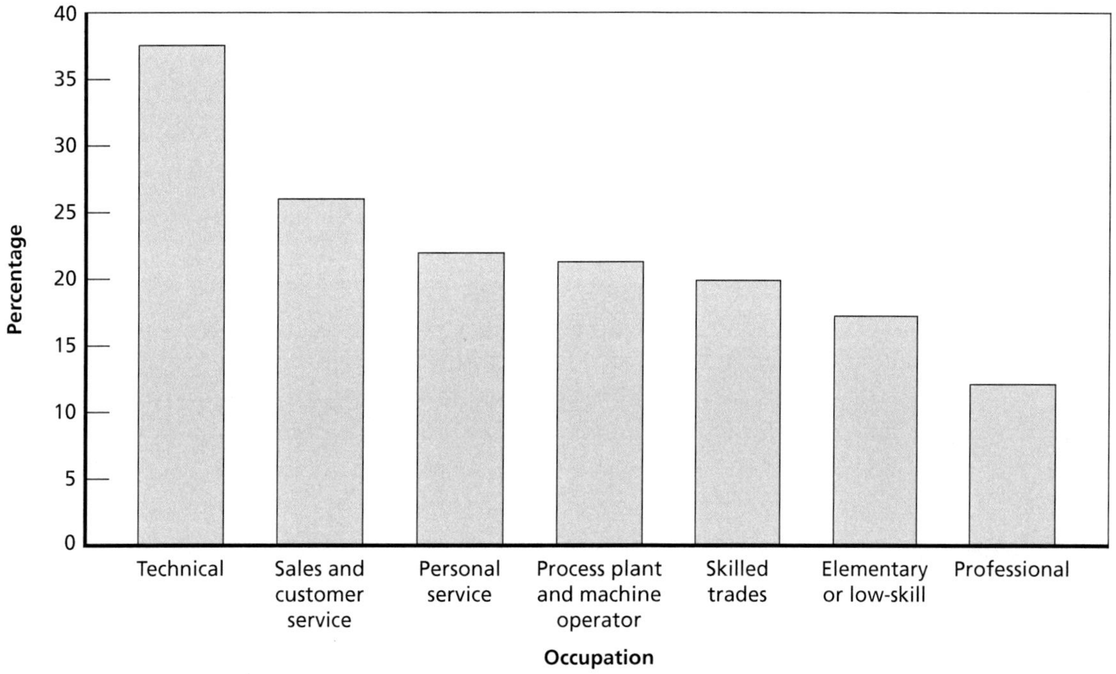

SOURCES: RAND Survey of Business Establishments (2012).
NOTE: N = 104. The survey question was, "Which of the following occupation categories is it difficult for you to hire locally?"
RAND *RR277-3.2*

[5] In the private sector, the KRLFS estimated a somewhat lower 10 percent share of employees as not from the KRI.

Figure 3.3
Average Percentage of Employee Not from the KRI, by Firm Size and Economic Sector, 2012

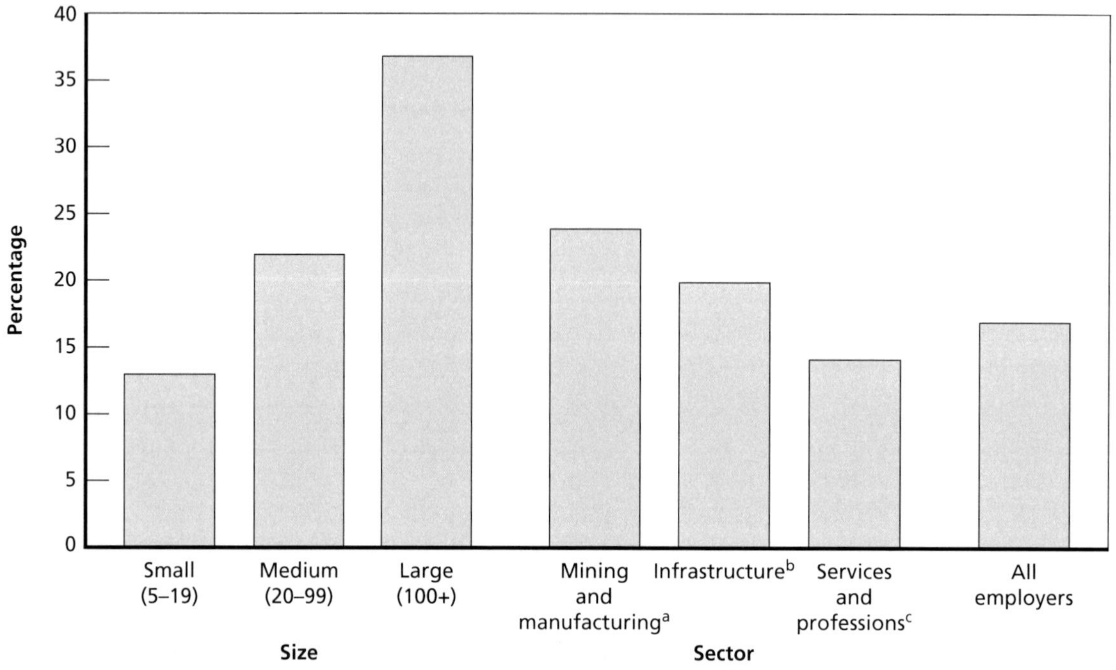

SOURCE: RAND Survey of Business Establishments (2012).
NOTE: N = 355. The survey question was, "What is the number of employees who are Nationals from the Kurdistan Region of Iraq; Nationals from other parts of Iraq outside of the KRI; Nationals of other countries?"
[a] Includes mining and manufacturing (International Standard Industrial Classification [ISIC] codes 5–33).
[b] Includes construction, transportation, and utilities (ISIC codes 35–43, 49–53, and 58–63).
[c] Includes wholesale and retail trade, real estate services, and tourism (ISIC codes 45–47, 55–56, 79, 64–66, 68–78, 80–82, 85–99).
RAND *RR277-3.3*

structure were significantly more than in the services and professions (e.g., wholesale and retail trade, tourism, real estate, and financial services).

Looking to the future, employers expected that about 20 percent of new hires would be non-KRI nationals. Large employers were significantly more likely than medium and small firms to say they would hire employees who are not from the KRI in the future. And employers in the mining and manufacturing and infrastructure sectors were more likely to say they would hire non-KRI employees than the services and professions sector.

Skills Demanded by KRI Employers

Which skills do KRI employers need of their workers? We asked employers to identify, from a list of 19 different skills, the three most important that they sought in applicants for jobs requiring a secondary education and for jobs requiring a tertiary education. Table 3.4 displays the frequency with which employers mentioned the three most important among the 19 skills.

Overall, the most frequently demanded skills were those required for interacting and communicating with customers (customer handling). This was particularly the case for jobs requiring a secondary education. Other common skills sought among applicants for jobs requiring a

Table 3.4
Percentage of Employers Rating Skills Among Their Three Most Important, by Level of Education Required for Job, 2012

Skill	Jobs Requiring a Secondary Education (ISCED 3)	Jobs Requiring a Tertiary Education (ISCED 5)
Reading, writing, numeracy, and IT		
General IT	17	16
Professional IT	8	10
Numeracy	8	21[a]
Reading	7	17[a]
Writing	8	17[a]
Foreign-language skills		
English	9	21[a]
Arabic	11	9
"Soft" skills		
Oral communications	29	20[a]
Written communications	32	19[a]
Customer handling	42	21[a]
Teamwork	15	10
Problem solving	8	6
Job-specific skills and experiences		
Specialized technical knowledge	6	18[a]
Practical technical experience	18	24
Management and administrative		
Management	11	15
Office administration	11	10
Work ethic and attitudes		
Willingness to work hard	32	19[a]
Willingness to learn	13	11
Positive attitude	15	18

SOURCE: RAND Survey of Business Establishments (2012).

NOTE: N = 360. The survey question was, "Thinking about jobs that require a 'level of education,' what are the three most important skills or aptitudes that you look for in a job applicant?"

[a] Indicates that the difference in the frequency the skill is included among the top three desired for jobs requiring tertiary education is significantly different from the frequency it is included for jobs requiring a secondary education at the 1 percent level.

secondary education were a willingness to work hard as well as written and oral communications. Commonly sought skills among applicants for jobs requiring a tertiary education were practical technical experience, numeracy, and English.

Below, we discuss employer responses regarding groupings of related skills.

Reading, Writing, and IT User Skills

Reading and writing skills are significantly more important and valued for jobs requiring a tertiary education than for jobs requiring a secondary degree. In addition, 35 percent of employers we surveyed were dissatisfied with the writing and language skills of the local workforce.

Numeracy was also more emphasized for jobs requiring a tertiary than for those requiring a secondary education.

Foreign-language Skills

Many private-sector employers also sought foreign-language skills. Arabic skills are about equally desired in jobs requiring either a secondary or tertiary education, while English-language skills are more desired in jobs requiring a tertiary education than in jobs requiring a secondary education.

The need for English-language skills came up frequently in our employer interviews, especially among large and multinational firms in which a good command of English is highly sought after for new workers. Employers made statements such as:

> Anyone who can communicate in English has a leg up.

Others noted the importance of other languages in addition to English, particularly Arabic, and in some cases Turkish, for technical and vocational jobs. For instance, in a recent survey, more than 50 percent of car maintenance and more than 70 percent of telecommunication firms preferred personnel with English and Arabic skills (UNESCO and ICON Institute, 2012). As one employer stated:

> A majority of my workers do not speak Arabic and Turkish and English and those are needed. In all jobs you need to read instructions on the machines.

"Soft" Skills

Soft skills include oral communications, interpersonal skills, problem solving, teamwork, and an ability to interact and communicate with customers. The latter, as indicated earlier, is the most sought-after skill among employers seeking to fill jobs requiring a secondary or a tertiary education. Other important soft skills in jobs requiring a secondary or tertiary education include oral and written communication and teamwork. KRI employer emphasis on "soft skills" in our survey is consistent with increased emphasis placed on such skills as reported in studies of employers around the world reflecting international trends (Axmann, 2004; ILO, 2010a; Sondergaard and Murthi, 2012; ILO, 2010b; ILO, 2008; World Bank, 2010).

The UNESCO and ICON Institute (2012) survey also found that car maintenance and telecommunications firms emphasize the need for customer-handling skills, with most firms of each type desiring such skills in their employees. Firms interviewed for that study also saw the lack of hands-on practical skills as a main weakness among workers in the KRI, listing soft skills after that.

Our qualitative data confirm the survey findings. One employer stressed the need for individuals who can write correspondence, handle customers, and possess basic communications skills required in a professional workplace. Interviews also suggested dissatisfaction with the problem-solving and teamwork skills of workers. As one employer said:

> It took a long time to get them to think about teamwork.

Job-specific Skills and Experience

Specialized technical knowledge, as expected, was considered more important for jobs requiring a tertiary education than for jobs requiring secondary education. But for both types of jobs, having acquired practical technical skills was equally important.

The UNESCO and ICON Institute (2012) study similarly found an even greater demand for practical workplace experience and for specialized technical knowledge in the car maintenance and telecommunication firms that they surveyed. Eighty percent of car maintenance and 45 percent of telecommunications firms indicated practical technical skills were required. But more telecommunications firms (80 percent) required specialized technical skills than car maintenance firms (54 percent). In addition, both type of firms considered hands-on and practical skills to be among the major weaknesses of employees in the KRI.

Our interviews provided further evidence of the specific technical weaknesses that employers perceive in KRI workers. One representative employer said:

> Workers require technical skills, and this is lacking in many of the local workers, including those in construction. There is a need for people with vocational and practical skills as well as engineers. The biggest challenge is not professional positions, but [in the] middle—workers who need technical skills, who work with their hands. Many of the graduates have very little practical skills to complement their academic training.

At the same time, our respondents suggested that physical work might not be attractive to students in the KRI. As one employer said:

> There is a cultural trend to go to university. Everyone wants to be a university graduate, and no one wants to be a carpenter or a laborer.

Management and Office Administration

Management skills broadly encompass the ability to organize a workforce and a business; to identify, prioritize, and delegate tasks appropriately; and to ensure an enterprise's smooth operations. Office administration is a related set of skills with more emphasis on organizing work, recordkeeping, logistics, and other administrative tasks.

Management skills are somewhat more important to employers than office administrative skills for jobs requiring a tertiary education. A common theme in many of our interviews was the lack of skills in modern management methods—the knowledge needed to organize and structure a company; arrange the lines of control; communicate across different departments within a company; and delegate tasks. As one employer stated, "There is no concept of management."

Work Ethic and Attitude Toward Work

A willingness to work hard was among the qualities employers desired among applicants for jobs requiring either a secondary or a tertiary education. We also asked employers whether they were satisfied with the work ethic and the attitudes toward work of their KRI workers. About 30 percent expressed dissatisfaction with the work ethic of KRI workers, and 18 percent expressed dissatisfaction with the employees' attitudes toward work.

In our interviews, several employers mentioned problems of a poor work ethic and a lack of willingness by KRI employees. Illustrating this concern, one employer stated,

> The issue is motivation—even in the private sector, they act like they work for the public sector.

Employer-Provided Training and Obstacles

Some of the employers we surveyed sought to overcome their employees' lack of preparation for work. About one in five employers reported that they provided some form of training to their employees, which is low compared to international practice.[6] The most common types of training these employers provided included practical training; vocational or trade training; training in problem solving; and training in customer handling (Figure 3.4). Less than one percent of employers provided training in foreign languages (Arabic or English).

As shown in Figure 3.5, 24 percent of employers reported encountering obstacles to providing training, with the most common obstacle being a lack of funds. Also mentioned with some frequency were the employer's inability to spare staff time and the lack of training providers available in the skills needed. The KRG should further investigate the state of training in the private sector and whether it calls for further action to provide training to employees as a way of raising the skills of the current and future workforce.

Summary

About half of the employed population is currently working for the government. Given that the KRG seeks to reduce its share of total employment, we can expect that future employment growth will take place primarily in the private sector. Within the private sector, future growth is expected to take place primarily in the service (retail, hotel, and tourism), wholesale, and transportation sectors, while construction can be expected to maintain its 25-percent share of the private KRI economy.

---

[6] The World Bank collects data on training offered by firms for full-time employees. Across countries for which this information was collected, 42 percent offered training between 2002 and 2010. In 2009 alone, 36 percent of firms provided some form of training. For that year, the range was from 5 percent of firms in Indonesia to 80 percent of firms in Samoa (World Bank, 2011).

Figure 3.4
Percentage of Employers Providing Training to Their Employees, by Type of Training Provided, 2012

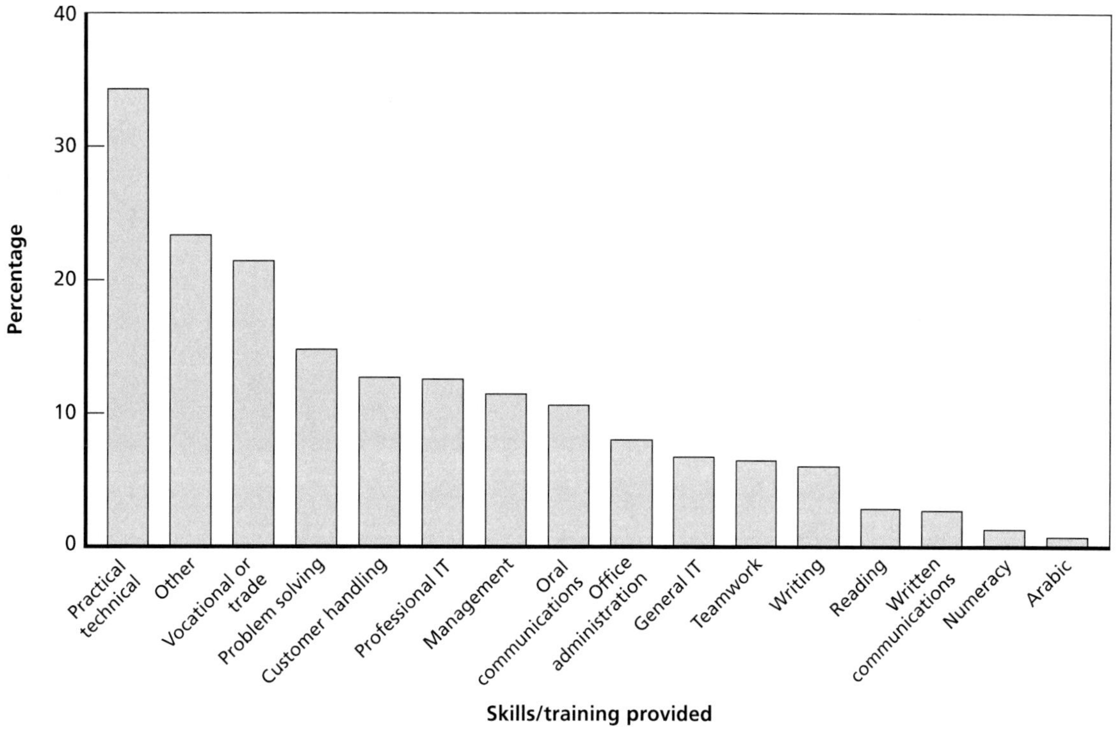

SOURCE: RAND Survey of Business Establishments (2012).
NOTE: N = 73. The survey question was, "What kinds of formal training are offered to employees?"
RAND *RR277-3.4*

Current employment patterns and expected employment growth suggest that secondary vocational education could play a significant role in preparing secondary students for the labor market. Nearly three-fourths of jobs in the private sector are in occupations—services and sales, skilled agricultural, craft and related trades, plant, machine operators and assemblers, and clerical support positions—for which secondary vocational education may provide an adequate preparation.

More than one-third of employers we surveyed said that secondary school graduates (both general and vocational) were ill prepared to join the workforce. They most often identified a lack of experience and of appropriate technical skills as major barriers to their hiring locally. Occupations that employers had difficulties hiring for included technicians, process plant and machine operators, sales and customer service, and some skilled trades. In the average firm surveyed, non-KRI nationals made up 17 percent of its total labor force.

Employers also identified a range of "soft" skills as lacking in graduates from secondary and tertiary education. These included oral and written communication, customer handling, teamwork skills, and a general willingness to work hard. Also notable for jobs that require a tertiary education were languages (English and Arabic) and IT skills.

Most employers surveyed did not provide training to their employees, but those that did tended to provide them in specialized skills related to the job. Less frequently provided was training in the "soft" skills and languages, suggesting that employers expect their hires to pos-

Figure 3.5
Percentage of Employers Citing Barriers to Providing Training, by Type of Barrier, 2012

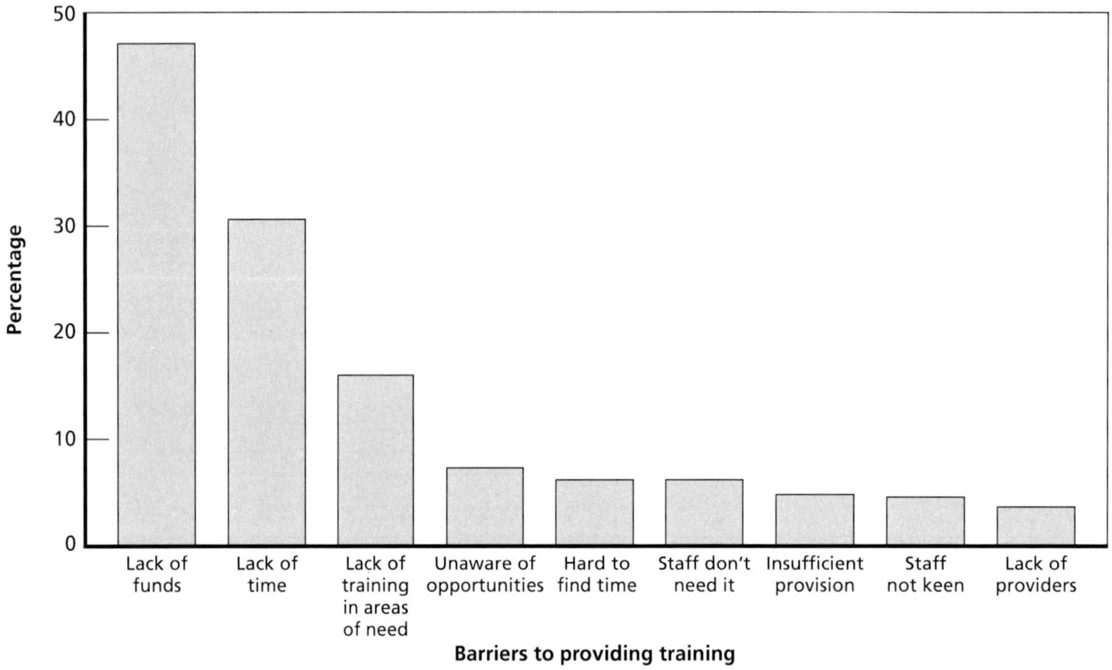

SOURCE: RAND Survey of Business Establishments (2012).
NOTE: N = 69. The survey question was, "What barriers have been preventing your organization from providing more training for employees at this location?"
RAND *RR277-3.5*

sess these skills prior to seeking a job. A lack of resources and time were the most frequent reasons employers cited for not providing training to their workforce.

CHAPTER FOUR

International TVET Policies and Practices

The Kurdistan Region—Iraq is not unique in its need to develop successful TVET programs. Several countries have developed such successful programs and use them to develop their workforces and meet other societal goals.

In this chapter, we present findings from a review of selected case-study countries (Germany, Finland, Jordan, Korea, Tunisia, and Turkey) and international literature on TVET systems and programs. In selecting these countries, we sought to represent a variety of TVET models in countries with highly regarded TVET systems, in developed and developing countries (including countries in the Middle East), and with populations similar in size to the KRI.[1]

We first provide a general overview of why countries invest in vocational education and how they structure vocational education within the broader education system. We then describe the key components of TVET systems, as identified in the literature, and provide examples of how different countries address these components. These examples provide evidence regarding steps the KRI could take toward improving its TVET system. We focus on secondary vocational education (ISCED 3). We also note how elements of TVET systems in other countries compare to the current situation in the KRI.

Overview of Objectives and Systems

In developing their TVET systems, countries need to first consider why and how they should support secondary vocational education. The goals for TVET will help shape what types of secondary vocational programs are provided and how they fit within the education system. Once they have decided that vocational education should be a component of secondary education, policymakers need to consider when and how it should be introduced and at what level of participation. Participation is a relevant indicator for TVET's attractiveness. TVET systems need to be perceived as attractive to stakeholders in order to achieve sufficient levels of participation and employer engagement. Below, we discuss what case studies of other countries indicate about TVET objectives, system structure, participation, and attractiveness.

Objectives

Countries provide technical and vocational education and training for multiple reasons. These include:

[1] A more complete and detailed report on these country case studies has been provided to the KRG in a separate document (Culbertson, Stasz, and Vernez, 2012).

- *Supporting the needs of the labor market and the economy.* This is a prime objective for most countries. There is a well-established relationship between skills and productivity both in theory and in empirical research. Human capital (including vocational skills) is one of the main determinates of labor productivity. The more skilled the labor force, the more firms are able to update their practices and products to address variations in demand. This makes the economy more flexible over time and increases the return on capital investment.
- *Supporting foreign investment.* Governments have an interest in improving the skills of the local labor force so that employers can be less reliant on foreign workers. Some portion of foreign workers' earnings are returned to their home countries and therefore lost to the local economy. A supply of skilled local workers also can support government incentives to foreign investors to hire local labor.
- *Supporting the development of private sector employment.* In developing economies, the government may have an interest in reducing the size of the government sector by encouraging the development of workforce skills that are particularly responsive to private employers' needs.
- *Supporting entrepreneurship.* TVET can help develop skills needed to build local entrepreneurship. This may be particularly useful in economies with a large informal sector and a predominance of small businesses.
- *Providing a recognized route to skill.* Not all youth want or are able to pursue higher education. TVET provides young people with an alternative way of obtaining marketable skills.

Overview of TVET Systems

Figure 4.1 provides a generic schematic overview of an education system, including TVET. Of course, each country has evolved a somewhat different set of institutions and requirements

Figure 4.1
Generic Overview of Education Systems

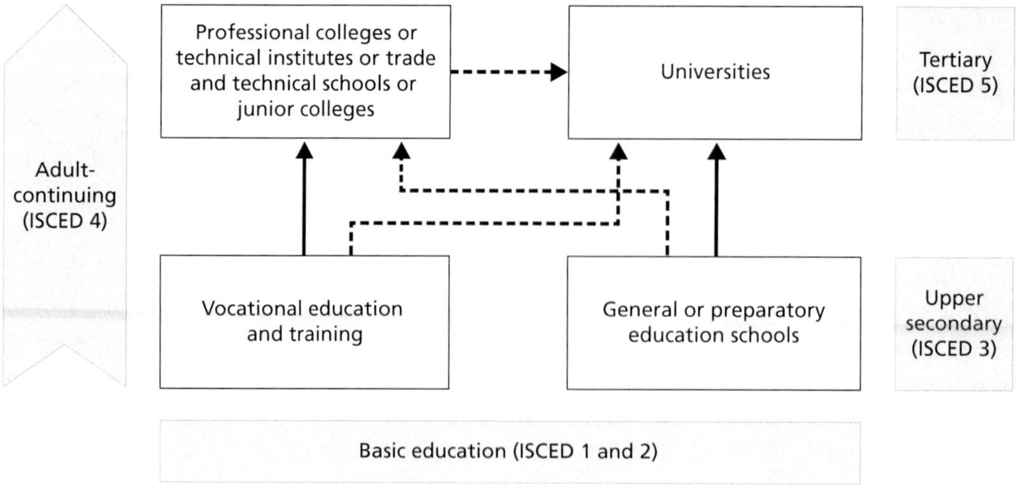

RAND *RR277-4.1*

for providing technical vocational education and training and for the progression of students across institutions and levels.

The entry into either secondary vocational education or general education may occur any time between the ages of 14 and 16 (at the end of grade 7 to grade 10). In many countries, this transition signals the end of compulsory education. Students may discontinue their education at this stage or, if they continue, may either choose their preferred program of study or be assigned to a program, usually based on their performance in compulsory education. Secondary vocational education may last from two to five years, with most programs lasting three or four years. Vocational education may be either school-based or work-based. Many countries have programs that incorporate both school and work in vocational education, albeit in differing proportions. Successful secondary vocational education students usually receive a certificate or qualification after successfully passing a test or examination.

Eligibility to progress from secondary vocational to post-secondary education is most frequently automatic, as it is from general education to university. In some countries, additional requirements, such as the successful passage of an exam or aptitude test, are necessary to make this transition. The post-secondary form of technical education is most frequently school-based and may last from two to four years. It can encompass programs at the post-secondary non-tertiary and tertiary levels.[2]

Graduates of secondary general education also may have access to post-secondary vocational education, although some practical experience may be required before enrollment. By contrast, TVET graduates rarely have automatic access to general university education. In most countries where it is even feasible, students are required to take additional courses or meet some aptitude requirements. The transition from secondary to tertiary level is smoother for those countries with an established TVET system at that level (e.g., polytechnic universities in Finland).

In addition to formal education, most TVET systems provide continuing vocational education through various programs that target adults without prior vocational training who are seeking to upgrade their technical skills or who have left school without any qualifications.

Participation in Technical and Vocational Education

Secondary Vocational Education

The role of TVET in preparing secondary students for the labor market and tertiary education is quite variable. In 2010, participation of secondary students in vocational education (ISCED 3) exceeded 50 percent, mainly in European countries including Finland and Germany, but also in other countries such as Australia and Egypt. Elsewhere, including in most Asian, Latin American, and Middle Eastern countries, secondary vocational education has an important but less dominant role. For instance, 45 percent of secondary students were enrolled in vocational education in Turkey in 2010; 32 percent in Lebanon; and 24 percent in Korea. Twelve percent of secondary students participated in vocational education in Jordan, and 11 percent participated in Tunisia (Figure 4.2). Participation in the KRI is much lower, at about 3 percent.

---

[2] The European Centre for the Development of Vocational Training (Cedefop) defines post-secondary non-tertiary education as programs that straddle the boundary between upper secondary and tertiary education. They serve to broaden the knowledge of secondary graduates and are designed to prepare students for studies at the first stage of tertiary education (university) or for labor-market entry. They do not lead to a tertiary qualification.

Figure 4.2
Percentage of Secondary Students in Vocational Education (ISCED 3), by Selected Countries, 2010

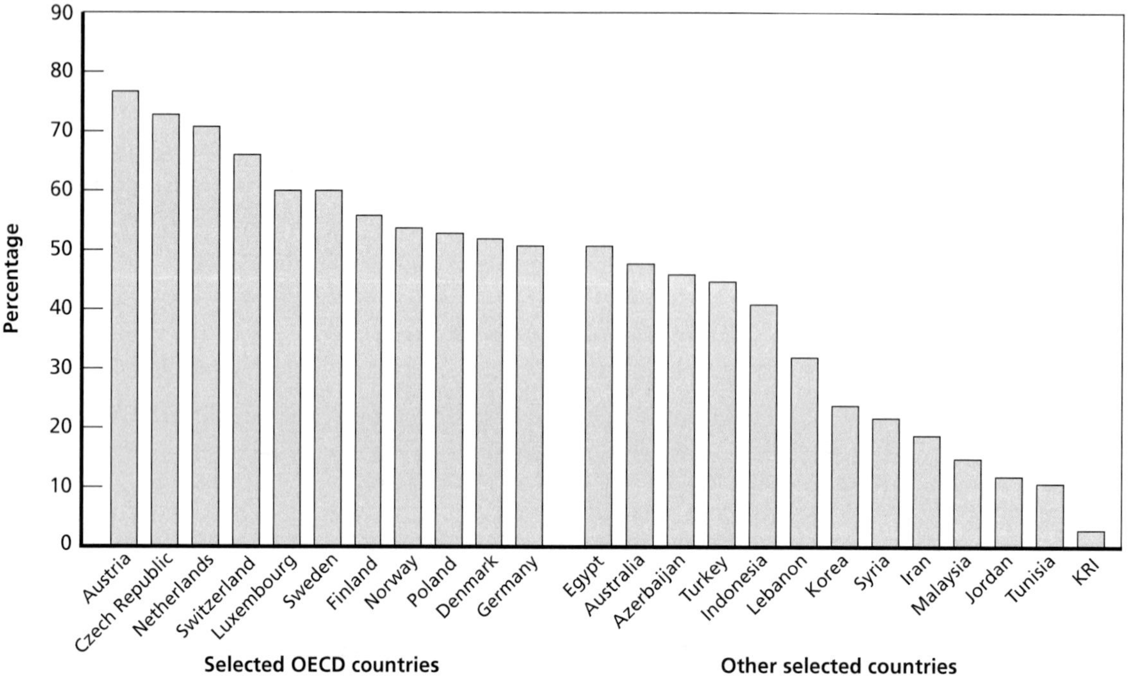

SOURCE: UNESCO Institute of Statistics (2012).
RAND *RR277-4.2*

Female participation in secondary vocational education typically ranges between 40 and 47 percent. Among our case-study countries in 2010, it ranged from a high of 47 percent of secondary vocational students in Finland to a low of 34 percent in Tunisia (Figure 4.3).

Post-Secondary TVET Education

Countries with high participation in secondary vocational education tend to also provide a range of TVET programs at the post-secondary non-tertiary level (ISCED 4) and at the tertiary level (ISCED 5). In Germany, for example, 74 percent of students in post-secondary non-tertiary programs were enrolled in TVET in 2012; enrollment in TVET as a proportion of tertiary students was 15 percent. In Turkey, 45 percent of students in tertiary education are enrolled in technical education. Most Korean secondary vocational students continued into tertiary education; in 2007, 43 percent transferred to junior colleges and 25 percent to university. In the KRI and Jordan, however, TVET enrollment is more concentrated at the tertiary level. In Jordan, 25 percent of tertiary students participated in 2008 in technical education, in comparison to around 15 percent at secondary. As discussed in Chapter Two, the bulk of TVET provision in the KRI is at the tertiary level, with, about one-third of students in tertiary education enrolled in technical education programs at technical institutes or technical colleges.

Attractiveness of TVET

The attractiveness of TVET education relative to general education varies considerably in the countries we reviewed. A recent survey found that most people in Germany and Finland think that vocational education and training has a positive image in the country (Eurobarometer,

Figure 4.3
Percentage of Secondary Vocational (ISCED 3) Students Who Are Female, by Selected Countries, 2010

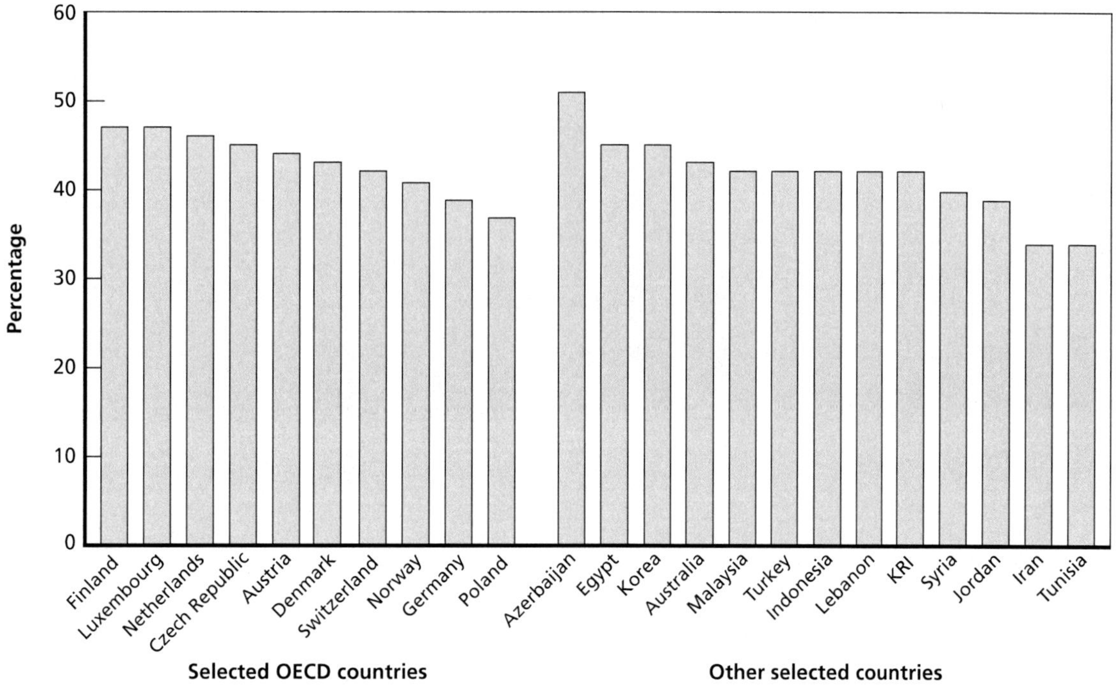

SOURCE: UNESCO Institute of Statistics (2012).
RAND *RR277-4.3*

2011). In Finland, survey respondents are more likely to recommend vocational education over general education to a young person entering secondary education, but in Germany, the reverse is true. This difference may be related to opportunities for higher education. In Germany, access to higher education for graduates of secondary vocational education is extremely limited, while in Finland the polytechnics and universities are open to all secondary graduates, both vocational and general education.

In Jordan, Korea, Tunisia, and Turkey, vocational education is perceived as less attractive than general education. In Jordan, lower-performing secondary students are assigned to vocational education, which promotes a negative view of this path. In Tunisia and Turkey, secondary vocational education mainly is the choice of students who failed to enroll in a general school because of relatively poor performance. The image of secondary vocational education in the KRI also is generally negative and tied to lower performance.

Making secondary vocational education more attractive is an important policy goal in many countries. Although there is no specific formula for increasing its attractiveness, research and practice indicate that improving the quality of vocational programs is key. Several conditions may make vocational education more attractive to learners. These include developing qualifications that have currency in the labor market; access to other education and training opportunities, including tertiary education; providing reliable information and career guidance services; and ensuring quality and relevance (Watters, 2009). Indeed, policies to increase attractiveness often are directed at improving these aspects of secondary vocational education (Guthrie et al., 2012).

Components of Education Systems

TVET systems and education systems in general have several common components (OECD, 2010; Watters, 2009; Sweet, 2009; ETF/WB, 2005; El Sawy, Farr, and Nerewa, 2012). These include:

- governance
- involvement of employers and other social partners[3]
- finance
- occupational offerings
- occupational demand and skill forecasting
- delivery methods
- curriculum
- student admission, progression, and graduation requirements
- guidance and counseling
- teacher and trainer qualifications
- quality assurance.

Although we discuss these components separately, in practice they may be interdependent. It may be difficult to transfer specific practices or policies across countries. Rather, implementation will depend on context, not least the often fast-changing needs of the economy and the preferences of students. Examples from the country case studies are offered to show the range of policies and practices that are being implemented, which may suggest a way forward for the development of TVET in the KRI.

Governance

The governance system sets forth the division of TVET's responsibilities at various levels—national, regional, and local entities—and the legal framework under which TVET is provided.

In the KRI, as earlier noted, governance of secondary vocational education (ISCED 3) is entrusted to the Ministry of Education, while the Ministry of Higher Education and Research oversees tertiary technical education (ISCED 5). The Ministry of Labor and Social Affairs has oversight of adult technical education (ISCED 4). There is little collaboration among these three levels. Elsewhere at the national level, most countries tend to place governance of their secondary and post-secondary TVET systems under one ministry. Of the countries we reviewed in depth, this is the case in Finland, Turkey and Tunisia. Korea, however, divides the jurisdiction of TVET between the Ministry of Education; Science and Technology, which is responsible for secondary vocational education; and the Ministry of Employment and Labor, which is responsible for the tertiary polytechnic colleges. There is little coordination between the two systems. Jordan has one vocational stream at the secondary and tertiary levels under the Ministry of Education and another stream overseen by the Ministry of Labor. In a recent reform, Jordan established the Employment and Technical and Vocational Education and Training Council as an umbrella governing body over all TVET programs.

---

[3] The term social partners is used commonly in TVET and can include employers, trade unions, teacher unions/groups, student unions, industry sector bodies, and the like.

While decision-making and administration of TVET systems is centralized in Jordan, Korea, Tunisia, and Turkey, Finland and Germany give extensive autonomy to local or regional authorities and schools for the content and the design of the TVET curriculum. These local authorities, however, are guided by national-level curriculum and standards for TVET.

Involvement of Employers and Other Social Partners

The involvement of social partners (employers, sector bodies, trade unions, student unions) is considered crucial to ensuring the labor-market relevance of TVET programs. Social partners' participation is legislated in some countries, which in effect gives them a formal role in TVET governance. The extent of participation and influence of social partners varies in the countries reviewed. In the KRI, there are no institutional mechanisms to engage the participation of social partners in TVET. Other nations, however, have several such mechanisms.

In Finland, for instance, social partners participate through National Tripartite Committees for each occupational field, with a responsibility to plan and develop vocational requirements. Jordan's employment and technical and vocational education and training (E-TVET) Council enables industry, trade unions, and training providers to play a role in TVET. Turkey has National and Provincial Education Boards to advise on curriculum, content of practical training, number of students to enroll in specified occupations, required vocational competencies, and student qualification examination.

The German system features collaborative public-private sector involvement at all levels of government in TVET design and operations. The influence of social partners in this is equal to that of the government.[4] At the national level, two ministries help set the framework for TVET: the Federal Ministry of Economics and Technology recognizes training occupations and issues training regulations, and the Standing Conference of Ministers of Education and Cultural Affairs issues the framework for the curricula. The Federal Institute for Vocational Education and Training (BIBB), with membership of all stakeholders, advises on standards and regulations. At the *Länder* (state) level, committees for vocational education with equal representation of employers, employees, and *Länder* authorities advise on issues such as providing support for disadvantaged youth and additional qualifications requiring school training. Competent bodies at the regional level include representation from the chambers of industry and commerce and crafts. They monitor training in enterprises, advise training enterprises, establish and maintain a list of training contracts, and design and hold final student examinations. At the sector and enterprise level, works councils exercise their influence through collective bargaining around pay for apprentices and planning and implementing their training.

Korea has only recently moved to involve social partners in TVET policy and curriculum design through the formation of sector councils. Trade unions are not participating in those councils, and employers have shown little interest thus far in school-industry initiatives. Nevertheless, partnerships between local schools and firms do occur on an adhoc basis. Similarly, Tunisia has recently set up national advisory and management bodies giving employers and unions a formal, stronger role in the management of vocational education.

---

[4] Switzerland has a similar collaborative system.

Finance

How the TVET system is financed can affect access to vocational education and the degree of participation and involvement of social partners. Typically, TVET systems either are fully funded by the public, as in the KRI, or partially funded by the public, with varying levels of contributions by employers or students.

TVET is fully funded by the public in Finland, with 42 percent nationally funded and 58 percent locally funded by the municipalities. In Jordan, 85 percent is publicly funded, including a 1 percent training-tax levy on all employers, and 15 percent of funding raised privately through testing fees. In Tunisia and Turkey, the public mostly funds TVET. In Tunisia, employers contribute 1 or 2 percent of their wage bill, depending on their type of enterprise. In Turkey, employers contribute 1 percent of income taxes to an Apprenticeship, Vocational, and Technical Education Development and Promotion Fund. Employers also contribute money for training equipment and material, with amounts varying by the enterprise's gross payroll, number of employees, and sector.

In Korea, the central government finances 80 percent of TVET programs, with the remaining funds contributed by local authorities or raised through school admission fees and tuition. Private vocational education and training schools, which are numerous in Korea, receive a small amount of government funding and subsidies,[5] but are primarily funded through tuition and fees and support from private donors and organizations.

In Germany, financing of secondary vocational programs is based on a system of mixed public and private financing, reflecting its public-private partnership approach. All levels of government—federal, *Länder*, and local—contribute, as do companies, unions, Chambers, and associations. The school-based component of the apprenticeship is financed by the *Länder* (for teacher training and teachers' pay) and by local authorities (for school construction, maintenance and renovation of school buildings, ongoing management, and procurement of teaching and learning resources). Enterprises contribute the on-the-job training component of apprentices' training and their wages. In 2007, 84 percent of the cost of the dual system was borne by employers providing training, with the remainder covered by the *Länder* (Hoeckel and Schwartz, 2010).

Occupational Offerings

For which occupations should TVET be provided, and at what levels? While there is no absolute answer to this question, all systems need mechanisms to balance student preferences for TVET and labor-market needs. The KRI offers only 14 occupational options in secondary vocational education, far fewer than the number offered in the case study countries.

Regardless of the share of secondary students participating in vocational education, most countries offer more than 100 occupations. In Germany, for example, more than half of secondary students are enrolled in secondary vocational education with 349 occupational offerings, whereas Jordan and Tunisia, where about 11 percent of secondary students participate in vocational education, offer 200 and 150 occupations, respectively (Table 4.1).[6]

---

[5] In Korea, about half of secondary schools are private.

[6] Note that high numbers do not necessarily relate to quality. Finland, for example, has reduced the number of secondary programs and post-secondary specializations to provide greater breadth within programs and improve transitions between different levels of vocational education and training (VET).

Table 4.1
Percentage of Students in Secondary Vocational Education (ISCED 3) and Number of Occupational Offerings in Selected Countries, 2010

Country	Number of Occupational Offerings	Percentage of Students in Secondary Vocational Education (ISCED 3)
Germany	349	58
Switzerland	250	64
Austria	245	72
Jordan	200	12
Turkey	197	64
Finland	187	71
Tunisia	150	11
Norway	112	50
KRI	14	3

SOURCES: Cedefop, 2012; Eurobarometer, 2011.

TVET offerings may cover multiple employment sectors and jobs within them, including the construction trades, transport, commercial, financial, health care, agricultural, design, mechanical, energy, electronics, communications, and food preparation areas. About half of the TVET students in Finland, for example, were in the technology and transport area, with welfare and health-related occupations and tourism, and catering and home economics occupations each accounting for 10 to 16 percent of enrollments.

In Switzerland, the ten occupational areas with the largest number of enrolled students in 2009 were commercial employee, retail employee, health-care worker, social-care worker, cook, electrician, IT worker, hairdresser, automobile mechanic, and logistician. Bricklayer, carpenter and painter also were among the 15 top occupations in demand by students (Federal Office for Professional Education and Technology, 2011).

Occupational Demand and Skills Forecasting

Although the KRI has no formal or informal process to assess labor market needs and add, subtract, or alter the number and content of occupational programs, other countries use a variety of tools to assess the demand for skills and to determine the kinds of training to provide. These include:

- surveys of employers to assess the quality of graduates
- surveys of employers to assess skill needs by occupations, and changes in skill demands
- surveys of recent graduates to assess the adequacy of their skills and the jobs they obtained
- analyses of job advertisements to help determine demand for jobs by sector and type of occupations
- projections of occupational and qualifications requirements to anticipate future demand and skill needs.

The information generated is necessary to determine the kinds of occupational training to provide, help make changes in training curricula, guide the choices students make, and otherwise determine desirable improvements in TVET policy and practices.

For example, the Finnish National Board of Education developed the "Mitenna Model," based on statistical data, for anticipating vocational training and skills needs nationally and regionally. The Foresight Network, set up in 2005, includes representatives from all ministries and the Prime Minister's Office. The Network coordinates ministries' foresight activities, promotes such activities at the regional level, and ensures that the outcomes inform policymaking. It organizes an annual Foresight Forum, which functions as a medium for discussion among ministries, regional and local governments, and labor market organizations. Both aim to improve the quality and relevance of TVET by giving reliable and useful information about the sort and amount of education needed to fulfill future skills needs and to safeguard access to skilled labor. The information is used to steer TVET by targeting student intake, detecting bottlenecks in the labor force, and identifying early any oversupply. The results benefit the students through career guidance and inform the Development Plan for Education and Research, which the government produces every four years (Watters, 2009).

In 1999, Germany established a system for anticipating skill needs. The main part of this initiative is the research network "Early Identification of Skills Needs in the Network" (*FreQueNz*). It includes several research institutions, the Federal Institute for Vocational Education and Training (*BIBB*), the German Confederation of Trade Unions (*DGB*) and the German Employers' Organization for Vocational Training (*KWB*). The aim of *FreQueNz* is the timely identification of future skills needs and the evaluation of their impact on TVET. The emphasis is on recording changes in the market to enable a more rapid reaction to occupational skills trends. The task is to use these requirements to derive or develop models for future skills and occupational profiles. The *Länder*, and several regions in different *Länder*, pursue their own region-specific activities for early identification (e.g., regional monitoring of qualification developments, surveys on skill needs).

Delivery Methods

Vocational education at the secondary level typically is provided in one of two ways. In the *school-based* approach, theory and practical experience are provided predominantly in classroom and workshop settings. Countries that use this method often require students to complete a work-based internship, which may vary from two to six months. The second method is *apprenticeship* or "*dual system*"[7] and combines classroom theoretical education with work-based training at an enterprise. Workplace learning is considered important because it can help students develop technical skills on modern equipment and "soft" skills through real-world experience (e.g., teamwork, communication, entrepreneurship, dealing with customers). It also may make it easier for students to find jobs (because their skills become known to employers), and help employers identify promising candidates. The OECD (2010) recommends that all vocational education and training systems include substantial workplace training.

The school-based method is the only method used in several countries, including Korea and Turkey among our case study countries. It is the dominant but not exclusive method in

---

[7] Some countries refer to the "alternance" method, combining periods in an educational institution or training center and in the workplace. Alternance schemes can take place on a weekly, monthly, or yearly basis. Depending on the country, participants may be contractually linked to the employer and receive a wage.

Figure 4.4
Percentage of Secondary Students in Secondary Vocational Programs (ISCED 3), by Type of Programs and in Selected Countries, 2006

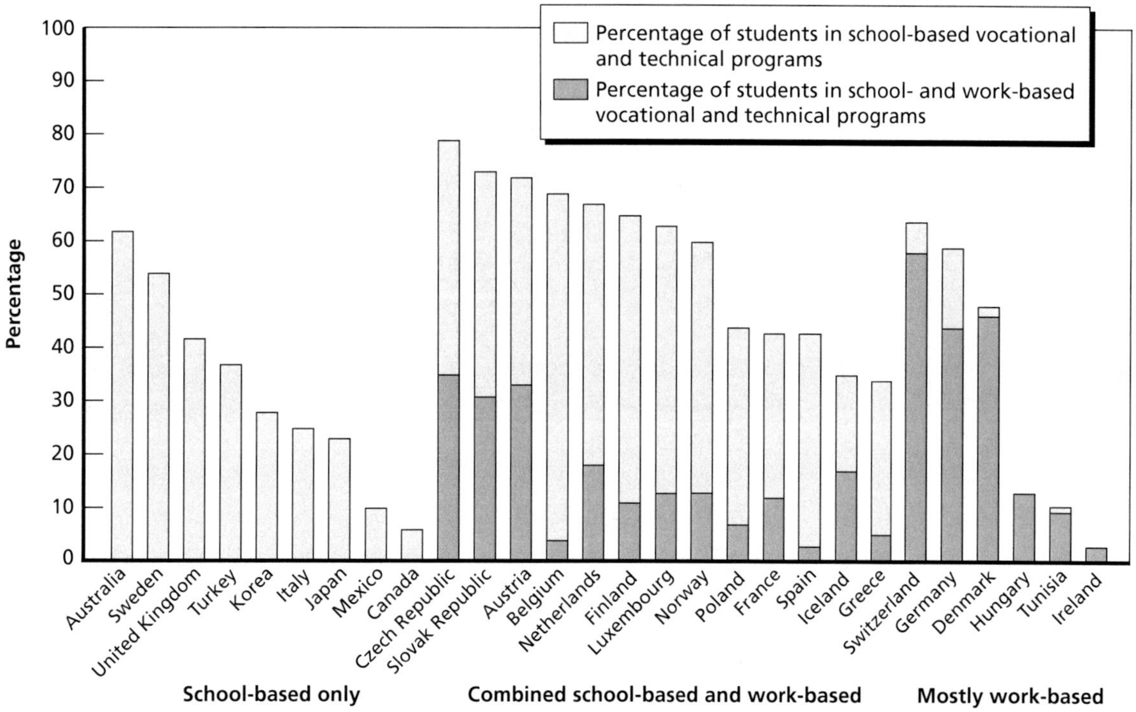

SOURCE: OECD (2010).
RAND *RR277-4.4*

Finland and many other countries. Mixed programs of school-based and apprenticeship training are the most common method in a handful of countries, including Germany and Tunisia (Figure 4.4).

In apprenticeships, students may attend school one or two days a week (Germany, Switzerland, Tunisia); for a sequence of segments each lasting some months on and off the job (Ireland); or in an arrangement in which students spend the first half of their vocational training in school and the second half in the workplace (Norway). While apprentices in most countries spend all of their employer-based training with one employer, Tunisia has implemented an "alternance" training program in which apprentices may be assigned to more than one employer over the course of their apprenticeship.

The existence of a *legal framework* that defines the rights and obligations of both trainees and employers is necessary for the success of apprenticeship programs. Apprenticeship contracts generally are drawn between the employer and the apprentice. The content of the contract may differ somewhat among countries, but in general it defines the obligations and rights of the apprentice and those of the employer, including the employer's obligations to employ and train the apprentice, pay wages, and ensure that the apprentice receives adequate facilities and supervision. In some countries, employers must submit a training plan and a probation period may be specified during which either party can terminate the agreement.

Typically, apprentices are entitled to an allowance or salary, which may range from 30 percent of prevailing wages in the occupation (Turkey) to as much as 80 percent (Finland). In

Jordan, apprentices are paid the minimum wage, and in Tunisia they begin at 30 percent of the minimum wage, with increments to reach 80 percent of minimum wage by the end of the apprenticeship period.

In some countries (Germany, Switzerland, and Austria), students are responsible for finding a company that will provide them with workplace training. In others (Hungary, Jordan, and Tunisia), students get help in finding an apprenticeship.[8]

In contrast to most other nations, the KRI only offers school-based secondary vocational programs. The only work experience students may receive is a two-month internship, one month in the summer between the first and second years and one month between the second and third years. Students must find their own placement. The internships appear to be pro forma, with little supervision provided by teachers or employers.

Curriculum

Historically, vocational programs have been designed as preparation for a single occupation. In the 21st century, however, those entering the labor market need not only immediate job skills but also a range of competencies enabling them to change jobs and careers throughout their working life. In addition, some vocational education pathways have been designed with the expectation that students can continue to post-secondary studies, even to university level. This shift from narrow occupational training to broader preparation for work or further education has increased the general subjects included in a vocational program.

Most secondary vocational programs include literacy and numeracy requirements. In addition to technical skills, many aim to develop the "soft" skills that employers want, such as an ability to work in teams, communicate with customers, and think critically. In Finland, for example, the core curriculum includes an understanding of other countries and cultures; the promotion of standards and sustainable development; the use of information technology; entrepreneurship; high-quality and customer-focused activity; consumer skills; and the management of occupational health and safety. Although vocational studies typically still receive more time in curricula than general subjects, there is enough attention to academics to ensure that students are ready for post-secondary education or can reach readiness with a few extra studies (ReferNet, 2011).

In countries where social partners help determine the content of vocational programs and set the standards for assessment and qualification, vocational training is relevant to work, and graduates' qualifications have currency in the labor market. In addition, many countries have or are implementing qualification frameworks to make their vocational education and training systems more transparent. These frameworks allow the relative value of different qualifications to be more clearly recognized by students, employers, and other stakeholders by allocating qualifications to comparable levels.

In most countries we reviewed, the duration of secondary vocational education usually is the same regardless of the occupational focus. It ranges from one to two years in Jordan and Tunisia; three years in Finland, Germany, and Korea; and four years in Switzerland and

---

[8] One drawback of apprenticeship programs is that not all students who want to participate can find a placement, and they face the possibility of completing compulsory school without a marketable skill. Several approaches have been taken to address this problem. In Austria and Switzerland, these students are provided with school-based training or experience in simulated companies. Switzerland identifies students at risk of dropping out in the 7th and 8th grade or who cannot find an apprenticeship placement. Case managers are assigned to monitor these students and provide various forms of support in choosing a pathway or finding an apprenticeship place.

Turkey. In a few countries, including Switzerland, the length of vocational training may vary by occupation from two to four years.

At the tertiary level, the duration of technical study varies from one to four years depending on the institutions and occupational focus. In Jordan's community colleges, the duration of study is two years; in Finland's polytechnics, it is three to four years; while in Turkey's vocational higher schools, it is two years. In Korea's tertiary technical institutions, the duration of study is typically two years, but some programs can be one or three years.

In the KRI, secondary vocational programs are three years in duration and the time spent in general and vocational education is about evenly divided. The teaching of "soft" skills is not included in the current curriculum.

Student Admission, Progression, and Graduation Requirements

Admission and Progression

The decision to enroll in secondary vocational education either is the student's choice (Germany, Finland, Norway) or is based on academic performance or a school-administered entrance exam (Jordan, Korea, Tunisia). In the latter case, there is a tendency for lower-performing students to be allocated to vocational education. Switzerland has a somewhat hybrid secondary system providing student choice for its four-year apprenticeship program and a two-year program for lower-performing students. Similarly, Jordan assigns secondary students based on performance first to an academic stream, then to a vocational stream; the lowest-performing students are assigned to vocational training centers run by the Ministry of Labor. In places in which vocational education is seen as the educational program for "non-academic" students, its image usually suffers.

Pathways to technical or university education beyond secondary vocational education take many forms. Some have no further requirements other than the successful completion of secondary vocational education. Others place additional requirements on students. In Finland, secondary vocational qualification provides general eligibility to both tertiary technical education (polytechnics) and university without further examination. In Jordan, students in the academic and vocational streams are eligible for both university and community college, but students assigned to vocational training centers are not. Pathways in Germany have been devised to facilitate further education beyond apprenticeship, but very few apprentices have taken advantage of them.

It is more common for vocational students to face further requirements to matriculate to tertiary education. In Korea, for example, students who want to continue to tertiary education in any form must take and pass the Collegiate Scholastic Aptitude Test to become eligible for either tertiary technical education or university according to their scores.

Tunisia, having separated its secondary academic and TVET pathways under different ministries, established a stepwise vocational-education sequence. After two years of vocational education leading to a *Certificat d'Aptitude Professionnel*, students with the highest scores may enroll in another two-year program leading to a *Brevet de Technicien Professionnel (BTP)*. The BTP provides access to a further two-year program awarding a *Brevet de Technicien Superieur*.

In the KRI, secondary vocational education graduates take the ministerial exam, as general education students do, and may be assigned to tertiary technical education or university depending on their exam scores. Currently, few score high enough to be assigned to post-secondary academic or technical education. This lessens their job prospects. In addition, having few secondary vocational education graduates meet the requirements to continue to tertiary technical education limits the appeal of pursuing this track.

Graduation Requirements

In the KRI, secondary vocational students take a ministerial test that covers both general and vocational subjects. There is no national qualification framework for tertiary technical education.

Elsewhere, the degree to which graduation requirements meet employer standards can provide strong signals of the employability of vocational-education graduates. Graduation requirements take different forms and may be standardized and uniform at the national level or be institution-based, with or without national occupational standards or qualifications and participation of social partners.

Germany and Switzerland have standardized national assessment tests of students' performance based on a national qualification framework for each occupation, developed by equal representation of teachers, employers and trade unions. This "Chamber" exam tests students' occupation-specific competencies. Broader academic knowledge is assessed by the classroom teachers' evaluation of student performance throughout the apprenticeship. The employer adds a written evaluation of the apprentice's performance during the workplace portion of the apprenticeship.

In Finland, students are assessed through skills demonstrations, which are performance assessments devised and implemented in cooperation with employers. Students in Jordan take a standardized test, while in Tunisia each training center tests its respective students.

By contrast, student assessments in Korea are developed by individual vocational providers without the involvement of employers or alignment with the recently developed national qualifications. This is contributing to relatively high unemployment among graduates and is one reason why Korean employers hold secondary vocational education in low esteem.

Student Counseling and Guidance

Although the KRI provides no counseling and guidance services to students, student counseling and guidance is considered a key component of a TVET system, especially as careers diversify. Students need guidance at several points in their education: prior to deciding whether to pursue a vocational or general education program; to help decide which programs to pursue; and whether to continue to tertiary education. In most countries, students must make such choices between the ages of 14 and 16, as vocational programs typically start in the 9th or 10th grades.

While some countries (Jordan, Korea) have no or weak counseling and guidance systems, several others (Austria, Finland, Switzerland) integrate guidance into the curriculum at all levels of education from primary to tertiary and adult education. In Switzerland, for instance, career guidance is formally scheduled during the time of early compulsory education. In grades 7, 8, and 9 (intermediate school), students learn about career options and all teachers receive training so that they are knowledgeable about the labor market. Students also have access to freestanding centers for occupational information that provide information and counseling for all levels of the education and training system. In these centers, students can see generalist counselors and be directed to specialists with more knowledge about specific occupations. Printed and electronic sources of information are widely available, including information on labor market job prospects, salaries, and opportunities for advancement (OECD, 2010). Similar centers can also be found in Germany.

In Turkey, students in the last semester of primary school are required to take an introductory course on different professions and their associated standards of living to help them make an informed choice. Once in secondary school, 9th grade students take a two-hour weekly introduction and orientation course that provides an overview of both vocational and academic programs. Turkey has some 200 centers that oversee career guidance and psychological counseling in schools.

Teacher Preparation

Where teaching in vocational schools is divided between theoretical and practical courses, the requirements for teachers of occupational subjects focus less on formal tertiary technical or university education and more on occupational expertise and experience (e.g., craftsmen and foremen), complemented with courses in teaching methods and pedagogy. Table 4.2 lists secondary vocational education teacher qualifications for theory, practice, and experience for eight countries.

Table 4.2
Secondary Vocational Education (ISCED 3) Teacher Qualification Requirement in Selected Countries, by Type of Teachers

Country	IVET Teacher Qualifications Theory	IVET Teacher Qualifications Practice	Enterprise Trainer Qualifications
Austria	B.A. in teaching + 3-year experience in subject	Initial vocational education and training (IVET) diploma + craftsmen master exam + BA in teaching + 3-year practice in the occupation	Master craftsmen + 40 hours of pedagogical and basic legal knowledge + 6-year practical experience
Germany	B.A. + 3–12 months experience in subject + teaching course	Foremen or skilled worker + teaching practice and pedagogy course	Qualified in the occupation + knowledge of education theory + mandatory trainer aptitude test
Finland	B.A. + pedagogical training + 3-year experience in subject	Same as theory teacher	No requirements, but usually are skilled workers
Jordan	B.A. + one year post-graduate	Same as theory teacher	No requirement
Korea	4-year teaching certificate	Junior college in subject + pass teacher certificate exam	Not applicable
Norway	Trade or journeyman certificate + 3-year university or one year pedagogy and 2-year theoretical education in the trade or B.A. + 1-year pedagogy + 2 year work experience	Same as theory teacher	Not applicable
Tunisia	Baccalaureate + 2-year teacher training + certificate of aptitude + additional courses in subject area	Same as theory teacher	Enterprise responsible to train trainers
Turkey	M.A. + verbal and written exam + 3-year experience	Same as theory teacher	Not applicable

SOURCES: Hoeckel (2010) and Kuczera et al. (2008).

For trainers of apprentices in enterprises, subject-specific qualifications are required to the level of craftsmen, foremen, or skilled workers. In some countries, these qualifications may be complemented with a pedagogy course (Austria) or knowledge of education theory (Germany). In most countries (Austria, Germany, Finland, and Korea), secondary vocational teachers are required to participate in continuing education.

Vocational teachers in the KRI must now have a bachelor's degree, but are not required to have practical experience.

Quality Assurance

In addition to ensuring the participation of social partners' in setting and continuously updating high occupational standards, student qualification requirements, occupational curricula, and teacher certification standards, countries employ two additional strategies to ensure the quality of their vocational programs: (a) program or school accreditation, and (b) research.

Many countries use the inspection or accreditation of vocational schools or other vocational education and training providers to ensure quality. Tunisia, for example, has an inspection system, and the new education laws from 2008 stipulate that vocational training institutions (public and private) must be assessed periodically. Tunisia created the *Referentiel National de la Qualité de la Formation Professionnelle* (or National Framework for the Quality of Vocational Training) that includes intuitional self-assessment. In Germany, the entire school system is under the control of the state, with detailed provisions relating to quality laid out in the education acts and regulations of the *Länder*. Most *Länders* have additional regulations beyond the state for external and internal evaluation. Finland does not carry out inspections, but imposes a statutory duty on education providers to evaluate their own operations and to participate in external evaluation.

Research and evaluation also supports quality assurance and development in vocational education and training. In places in which responsibility for vocational education and training is spread among different government ministries or agencies, it can be difficult to collect, manage, and analyze relevant data. Some countries have established national centers to overcome this challenge. Germany, for example, has a well-developed and institutionalized research capacity for TVET, including the BIBB, and a national network of research centers that study different aspects of the system. The Finnish Education Evaluation Council provides independent evaluation of general, vocational, and adult education. In Jordan, the National Center on Human Resources Development (NCHRD) promotes and evaluates TVET and is developing a Human Resources Information System.

Summary

This chapter discussed policies and practices with regard to TVET in other countries, organized by a number of common components. It drew comparisons to the status of TVET in the KRI, the main points of which can be summarized as follows:

- Most countries tend to place governance of secondary and tertiary TVET under one ministry or coordinating agency, whereas the KRI divides responsibilities over three separate ministries that do not collaborate with one another.

- Most countries reviewed have mechanisms in place to engage employers and other social partners in TVET design and delivery; the KRI has no such employer involvement.
- TVET is fully publicly funded in the KRI, whereas other countries have various mechanisms for employers to contribute, such as by providing training (as in apprenticeships) or through tax levies.
- The KRI has only 14 different occupational offerings at the secondary level, while offerings in other countries reviewed range from around 100 to 350. This may partly reflect the low level of TVET participation in KRI, which stands at only 3 percent of secondary enrollment.
- Most countries have put in place institutions that use a variety of tools (e.g., surveys of employers and recent graduates, projections of labor demand) to assess demand for skills and determine the kinds of training to provide; KRI has no such capability.
- While it is recommended that any model of vocational education delivery include substantial workplace training, most countries, including the KRI, offer school-based TVET only with minimal opportunity for work internships with a company.
- The tendency is for a TVET curriculum to go beyond preparation for a job and to provide broader occupational skills, "soft" skills, and sufficient literacy and numeracy to advance to tertiary education or enable future career change. The evidence suggests that the KRI's program is not providing sufficient practical experience, technical skills, soft skills, or language skills.
- Countries are aiming to fashion secondary vocational education so that it is not a dead end but a pathway to employment and toward higher education, as this is key to increasing its attractiveness to students. The KRI, however, uses test scores at the secondary level to assign students to tertiary universities or technical institutes and does not provide the skills to compete and successfully meet these requirements. There are no separate assessments for vocational students or occupational standards by which to judge educational quality and demonstrate capacity to potential employers.
- Although guidance and counseling is considered essential for helping students make choices about their educational pursuits and careers, the KRI provides no such services.
- In most countries, secondary vocational teachers are required to have experience in their instructional field, but the KRI demands a baccalaureate degree only.
- The KRI lacks mechanisms that other countries employ to enhance quality assurance, such as inspection systems, independent accreditation, involvement of social partners, or research and evaluation.

CHAPTER FIVE

Recommended Roadmap for Improving TVET

The KRG is taking steps to expand and improve its TVET system. They include plans to create three large secondary vocational centers with places for 10,000 students in each. In this chapter, we present a roadmap to build on these efforts to make the system more responsive to both student and employer needs. We offer recommendations in support of the KRG's plans, drawing on our overview of KRI's current TVET system in Chapter Two, our survey and analysis of KRI employers and the skills they need in Chapter Three, and our review of international TVET policies and practices in Chapter Four. While we discuss all levels of TVET, we focus primarily on secondary vocational education and training.

The most-important lesson of the review of international practices is that there is no one best way to provide TVET. Rather, TVET systems are developed within the broader economic, social, and historical contexts—including demographic and labor-market trends, demand for qualifications, quality of education system, history of employer participation, and attractiveness of vocational training—that affect TVET delivery (Guthrie et al., 2012). We therefore tailor our recommendations based on effective international practices to the KRI's context, highlighting special considerations for expanding and improving the TVET system in the KRI.

The proposed steps are numerous, and will need to be implemented over time. In addition, they will entail a significant budget commitment.

Establish a Coordinated Governance Structure Across Ministries and Stakeholders

Regardless of the different ways to govern and oversee TVET systems, all countries reviewed for this study have moved toward achieving better coordination among national ministries, other levels of government, levels of education (secondary and tertiary), and social partners such as employers and trade unions.

To achieve better coordination of policy and practices across TVET components in the KRI, we recommend establishing a TVET Governing Council. This would include the KRG Ministers of Planning, Education, Higher Education and Scientific Research, Labor and Social Affairs (along with Directors General with responsibilities in TVET), and senior representatives of each of the governorates to provide local perspectives.

The TVET Governing Council would also include Occupation Committees with representation from employers, trade unions, teachers, and other social partners. These committees would help design TVET programs.

To support the Council, we further recommend establishing a TVET Governing Council General Secretariat, with responsibilities for employer relations, labor market research and data analysis, occupational standards and curriculum development, and communications. Figure 5.1 illustrates the proposed TVET governance structure.

The TVET Governing Council would have the authority to:

- coordinate policymaking and develop a TVET vision, objectives, and overall strategy
- develop policies in support of the strategy
- decide occupational offerings at all levels of TVET and create occupational standards and curricula for them
- coordinate progression from secondary to tertiary TVET, including curriculum and entrance requirements
- monitor trends in employer demands and evaluate the effectiveness of the TVET system.

The delivery and operations of the various levels of TVET programs would remain the responsibility of the ministries now holding those responsibilities.

The *Occupation Committees* established for each sector or group of related occupations would advise on occupational standards and curriculum requirements and be coordinated by the General Secretariat. Establishing the Occupation Committees may be challenging, as employers and other social partners do not currently have a role in TVET. An initial strategy might be to start with a few Occupation Committees for select industries, learn the most effective ways of managing them, and then expand the number of committees over time. External consultants or international organizations could be involved in the initial committee develop-

Figure 5.1
Proposed TVET Governance Structure

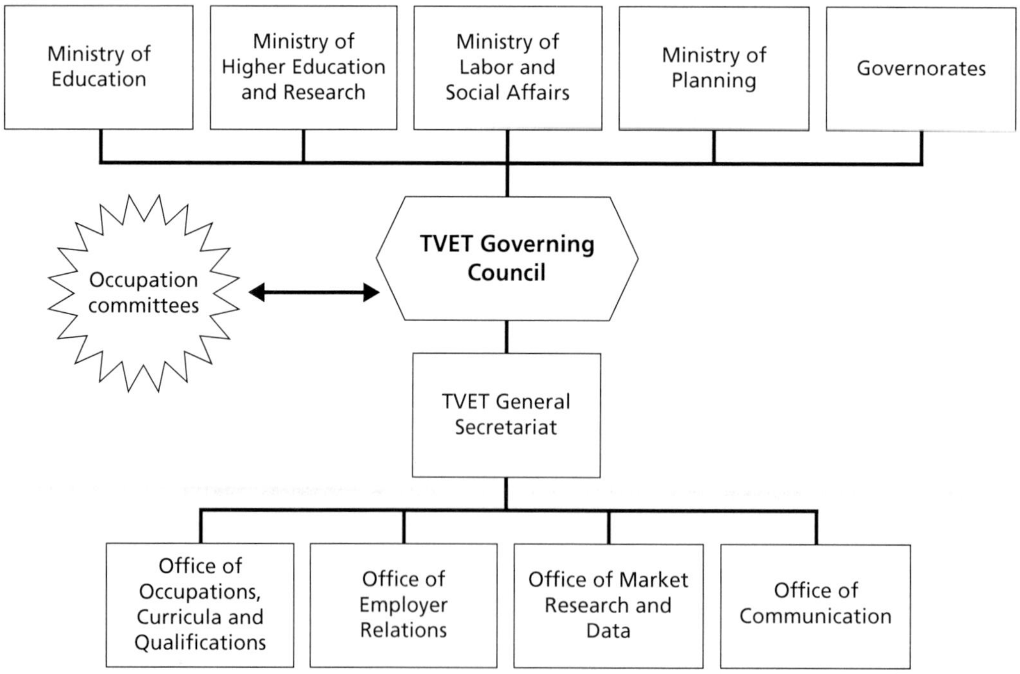

RAND *RR277-5.1*

ment stages. Each committee should not exceed 12 to 15 members, in order to encourage active participation by all members and minimize coordination costs. Based on our review of the KRI labor market, as well as data from the employer survey, we suggest starting with Occupation Committees for the energy, construction, telecommunications, and retail sectors.

The responsibilities of the four offices of the General Secretariat could include the following:

For the *Office of Occupations, Curricula, and Qualifications*:

- Provide information about occupational qualifications and curricula to the Governing Council.
- Coordinate the Occupation Committees.
- In collaboration with the Occupation Committees, develop occupational standards, curricula, and student qualification requirements for current and new occupations, both at the secondary and tertiary levels.
- Formulate competence-based qualifications requirements for various occupations or group of occupations.
- Establish requirements for the qualifications of teachers.
- Establish a framework for guidance and counseling services.

For the *Office of Employer Relations:*

- Develop relationships with employers to encourage their participation and that of other social partners in Occupation Committees.
- Negotiate standards, student and employer requirements, and a monitoring and evaluation framework for both secondary and post-secondary TVET internships.
- Create partnerships with employers to develop and pilot an apprenticeship model of training students.
- Gather additional input from employers about the skills and occupations for which they would like training to be provided.

For the *Office of Market Research and Data*:

- Develop data-gathering methods to determine current and future labor-market needs, including analysis of employment trends, surveys of employers, and surveys of students and graduates.
- Collect and disseminate data and research about the labor market and TVET to inform TVET Governing Council decisions, guidance and counseling services, and the public (employers, parents, and students).
- Coordinate with TVET centers to set up a system to collect data on employment rates of graduates and other important information on TVET outcomes.
- Develop a TVET information-management system, including a "dashboard" of important performance indicators (e.g., quality, graduate employment) that can be tracked over time.
- Coordinate with the KRSO in data gathering and analysis.

Having information about market needs and trends right away will be important for the MOE when designing the three new secondary vocational centers and selecting new occupational programs. We recommend that the MOE begin collecting data about market signals as an early priority, as it may take some time to fully establish the TVET governing council.

For the *Office of Communication*:

- Communicate to the public the importance of TVET to the economy and the plans of the KRG to expand access, improve quality, and provide routes to employment.
- Conduct an annual TVET Reform Conference to provide information about changes and plans, provide a forum for stakeholder input, and convey a sense of importance to the TVET reforms.
- Conduct ongoing communications with the public, employers, parents, schools, and students about the reforms and opportunities being created by the new system.
- Communicate positive outcomes of TVET (such as employment or transition to higher education) to improve its image.

Staffs of these various offices will have to develop over time the specialized expertise needed to carry out their missions. Initially, this may mean relying on expertise from external consultants, especially for developing occupational standards, designing curricula, and setting student qualification requirements.

Establishing the TVET Governing Council and its supporting General Secretariat could provide a central point for organizing, prioritizing, coordinating, and implementing the remaining recommendations below.

Develop Objectives for TVET in the KRI

The objectives that the KRG sets for its TVET system should shape its strategy, policies, and programs. A publicly available document could describe the objectives for KRI's programs. Such a document could help the KRG agree on plans for TVET, serve as a tool to build confidence of employers and foreign investors, and help to improve the image of TVET to students. We recommend the following objectives as central principles for the KRG's TVET development:

- promote quality, access, and relevance as core values
- support the needs of the labor market and the economy, including foreign investment, private-sector employment, and entrepreneurship
- provide individuals with the skills they need to contribute to the economy and to support themselves and their families
- establish recognized qualifications that signal acquired job skills as well as competences that enable changes in careers or progression to further education
- manage TVET in an integrated manner, with coordinated and open pathways among secondary, post-secondary, and adult TVET education, as well as with employment
- improve the image of TVET to increase its attractiveness to students, families, employers, and other stakeholders.

The recommendations in this chapter serve to support these objectives.

Enact TVET Legislation

Enacting legislation formalizing the TVET governance structure, granting it the appropriate authority, and defining the division of responsibilities between government, employers, and other social partners eventually will become desirable. Nearly all TVET systems have their governance, main features, and requirements coded in law to provide clarity and direction to stakeholders. A KRG TVET law might include:

- a description of the objectives of TVET for the KRI
- the governance structure and responsibilities, including the roles and responsibilities of the TVET Governing Council, General Secretariat, and Occupation Committees
- roles and responsibilities of social partners and employers, in particular with regard to on-the-job training and internships, input into occupational programs, and developing the technical parts of the curricula as well as occupational standards and student qualification requirements
- the authority of the TVET governing council to set KRI qualification standards
- other provisions that the KRG views as important to the functioning of a newly restructured TVET.

Increase Vocational Education Participation to 20 Percent of Secondary Students

The KRG is planning a threefold increase in participation of secondary students in vocational education (ISCED 3), with the three planned centers offering as many as 10,000 spaces each. The Ministry of Education also may set a goal for 20 percent of the secondary-school-age population to participate in vocational education over the next ten years, with further increases after that. We endorse this goal. This goal remains relatively modest, considering that participation of secondary students in vocational education in most OECD countries and some countries in the region, including Lebanon and Turkey, exceeds 30 percent. It would be somewhat higher than the level of participation in some other countries in the region, including Iran, Jordan, and Tunisia.

There are several reasons why the KRG should further expand the provision of secondary vocational education. First, as noted earlier, we estimate that secondary vocational education can provide sufficient preparation for about 70 percent of the jobs in the KRI labor market. Second, a large number of secondary students currently do not continue to tertiary education but rather enter the labor market without adequate skills to compete. As more students complete compulsory education to grade 9, offering a means to obtain marketable skills could encourage those students who otherwise would not have pursued secondary education to do so. Third, the KRI's economy is growing rapidly with both local and foreign companies expanding and needing better skilled employees to support this growth. With secondary vocational education providing an initial foundation of technical skills and knowledge, tertiary technical education could focus on providing more advanced and specialized skills.

Adopting this recommendation would require expanding secondary vocational education capacity to eventually serve more than 50,000 students. It would require:

- *Securing an adequate investment of public money to meet the goal.* Increasing participation in secondary vocational education requires appropriate budgets for buildings, equipment, and teachers.
- *Preparing qualified teachers.* Several thousand new teachers would be needed over the next 10 years. This will require plans to train these teachers.
- *Ensuring equipment and facilities are of appropriate quality, safe, and relevant.* TVET facilities and equipment in KRI are often in poor repair or not up-to-date. The three planned secondary vocational education facilities will help remedy this problem. Over time, plans will be needed to accommodate additional students, either by expanding those centers, renovating old facilities, or building new ones. Equipment will need to be appropriate and relevant; the best way to ensure relevance is to consult with employers through the Occupation Committees to determine the equipment and material needs for training.

Develop Occupation Standards and Set Student Qualification Requirements

Most countries with TVET systems assess the technical and practical proficiency of their students against nationally set qualifications standards. These standards often are developed with the input of employers, not only to ensure that graduates meet their needs but also to ensure more generally that students have acquired the skills necessary to compete in the labor market.

We recommend developing occupation specific and group of occupations standards that set new, more rigorous credentials for occupations offered through secondary, tertiary, and adult education TVET, with diplomas offered at different skill levels. The standards should be consistent across the KRI and designed by the Occupation Committees. As the Occupation Committees establish each new occupational program, they should develop the accompanying curriculum (see below) and student qualification requirements. The qualification requirements should be based on the occupational standards developed by each relevant Occupation Committee. Components of the student qualification requirements could include:

- a test of general skills
- an occupation-specific written test
- occupational skill demonstration
- passing grades in courses
- evidence of a satisfactory completion of a workplace internship.

Upgrade the Secondary Vocational Education Curriculum

The KRI's TVET curricula have not been updated for ten or more years. Now is an opportune time to update and improve its quality. Curriculum revisions for the secondary vocational education level should include:

- broadening general subjects at a similar level to the preparatory track
- upgrading current vocational curricula
- incorporating practical experience in the workplace.

Broadening General Subjects and Making Them Similar to the Preparatory Track

In the countries we reviewed, there is an increased emphasis on devoting time to general subjects, most particularly literacy, numeracy and languages, as well as imparting "soft" skills such as communication and teamwork. Similarly, in the KRI, employers indicated that TVET graduates should possess better numeracy and language skills, "soft skills," and skills in the use of IT.

To improve students' numeracy and language skills, we recommend that the curriculum content for the academic subjects of the secondary vocational education program should be the same as for the preparatory program. This also would help graduates of secondary vocational education pursue tertiary technical or university education if they wish. The vocational curriculum should not cut off pathways to further education or be viewed as a dead end. Teaching of soft skills—such as teamwork, interpersonal skills, critical thinking and problem solving, ability to work independently, time management, responsibility, work ethic, and handling of customers—could be added to the curriculum for many occupational offerings. Similarly, training in the use of information and computer technology applications, such as use of the Internet, Word, and Excel, could be added to the general subjects of selected occupational offerings, as determined by the relevant Occupation Committees.

Upgrading Current Vocational Curricula

As noted above, we recommend that the Occupation Committees be formed to update the curricula of current vocational offerings to today's requirements. These committees could take advantage of curricula developed or being developed by UNESCO, the British Council, German International Cooperation (GIZ), and otherwise already developed in other countries.

Upgrading Practical Workplace Experience

Most countries with well-developed TVET programs, including Germany, Norway, and Turkey, emphasize offering practical workplace experience as part of their curricula. KRI employers also say they would like TVET graduates to have more practical workplace experience than they currently do. Students may gain such experience through workshop-based programs, workplace internships, or apprenticeship programs.

First, in school-based programs, such as in the three new secondary vocational centers or in other TVET facilities, workshops could be designed to simulate the workplace environment. Such workshops could consider providing free or nominal-charge services to members of the community for any goods or services produced. For example, students in an auto-mechanic workshop could, under supervision of their teachers, repair the cars of community members.

A hairdressing workshop also might offer the services of its students to community members. Classroom-based vocational and training programs will continue to be the primary mode of secondary vocational education delivery for the foreseeable future, because there are not enough employers in the KRI with the capacity to provide workplace training for a sufficient number of occupations to meet student demand.

Internships are an additional way to provide practical experience in school-based programs. Although the KRI's TVET programs already require internships at the secondary and tertiary levels, they need to be more formally defined for both students and employers in order to be effective and ensure quality. A formal internship agreement among the school, student, and employer could specify the form of training the student will receive, the supervision that will be provided and by whom, and the responsibilities and rights of both student and employers. To encourage the participation of employers, subsidies or some other form of incentives could be provided. Counseling and Guidance Offices in the secondary vocational centers (below) could facilitate student placement in internships.

We recognize that in the near future, internship opportunities will be limited by the number of employers able to offer them. If insufficient internships are available, then TVET programs should ensure that students who cannot find a workplace internship are able to acquire similar practical experience in a workshop setting. As the system develops in ways that create value for employers—for example, by improving the quality of programs and their graduates—it may become easier to recruit employers to offer internships.

Third, even though the main form of TVET delivery in the KRI must continue to be school-based, we recommend undertaking pilot programs in which apprentices receive most of their training at a company. The TVET General Secretariat's Office of Employer Relations could identify a few occupations in which there is adequate capacity in a number of companies willing to initiate small apprenticeship programs. Models for apprenticeship can be found in many countries, and these can be consulted in initial stages to design the formal guidelines and requirements for apprenticeships in the KRI. As the program develops over time, it could expand to include apprenticeships for additional occupations.

Coordinate Progression from Secondary and Tertiary TVET Programs

A lack of opportunities to progress beyond the secondary level contributes to the negative view of vocational education in many countries, and this also is the case in the KRI. It will be important to remove barriers that prevent most current secondary vocational education graduates from continuing their technical education at tertiary technical institutes and universities.

As curricula are developed for secondary vocational schools, it will be necessary to revise technical-education curricula offered at tertiary technical institutes to ensure that they are of sufficient breadth and depth for students to progress to higher technician levels. The TVET Governing Council and Secretariat should coordinate the student-progression process from level to level, ensuring that students receiving diplomas from secondary vocational education have the skills needed to continue.

Expand Occupational Programs

Current or planned KRI occupational programs are not sufficient in number to meet the needs of the KRI economy, as noted earlier. Expanding the range of occupational programs not only would broaden the appeal of secondary vocational education to KRI students but also would make the system more responsive to the labor market. We recommend increasing the number of programs over the next ten years, based on assessments of market demand by the TVET Secretariat and Occupation Committees as well as on research conducted by the Office of Market Research and Data. As each new occupational offering is identified, the TVET Secretariat and relevant Occupation Committee should develop accompanying occupational standards, curriculum, and student qualification requirements as noted above.

As a starting point, we recommend that the Ministry of Education consult with the largest employers in the KRI on their needs for future employees, and establish programs to meet those needs. The growing sectors in which skilled personnel are needed and for which secondary vocational education offerings are not available include oil extraction and distribution, transport, tourism, construction, and the rapidly expanding service sector.

Set Additional Teacher Preparation Requirements and Create Plans to Develop Enough Qualified Teachers

Improving secondary vocational-teacher quality and numbers in the KRI will be a significant challenge. It will be especially important for vocational teachers and trainers to have relevant occupational qualifications and experience that they currently are not required to have. In addition, the KRI will need a large number of new teachers to staff the three planned new vocational centers. We propose the following measures to enhance teacher quality and numbers for current and new teachers of both the general curriculum (such as Kurdish, math, and English) and the vocational and technical courses.

First, the new secondary vocational centers could provide opportunities for current teachers of vocational subjects to gain up-to-date, practical experience in workplaces, perhaps by facilitating teacher visits and internships with local employers or exchange opportunities supported by international donors.

Second, program administrators could set requirements and programs to enhance the pedagogical skills of current general curriculum and vocational teachers who lack bachelor's degrees and for new hires lacking teacher training. Such programs could be developed in collaboration with teacher colleges. Our report on the KRI's K–12 education system has a set of recommendations for preparing these teachers (Vernez, Culbertson, and Constant, 2012).

Third, new requirements should be set for new teachers, both general and vocational. Teachers in the general subjects in the vocational program should have the same academic qualifications as general teachers in the secondary preparatory schools. Our report on the K–12 education system offers recommendations for these qualifications (Vernez, Culbertson, Constant, 2012). Teachers of vocational subjects should have either a diploma from one of the technical institutes or a bachelor's degree from a technical college. In addition, requirements for practical experience for new vocational teacher hires should be set. While secondary vocational centers could give hiring preference to candidates who already have a tertiary technical diploma and relevant work experience, the technical diploma requirement could be waived for teachers of the practical, occupation-specific courses until enough vocational teachers can be found who meet both education and work requirements.

Establish Offices at TVET Providers to Provide Student Counseling and Guidance

Most countries offer student counseling and guidance to students making decisions about which academic or vocational secondary school path to take and to students graduating and seeking jobs. The KRI provides no counseling and guidance services to students, so it will take some time to develop these services as a regular part of schooling.

As a starting point, we recommend setting up guidance offices at the three new secondary vocational facilities and at the Technical Education Institutes. At a minimum, these offices should employ counselors who are experienced in labor-market issues and who can call on a wide range of information to support students at key career-decision points. In coordination with the TVET Secretariat, these offices could eventually have responsibility for such activities as providing counseling to 9th grade students in the basic schools on how to make their choice of pursuing a vocational program of study; counseling students on their TVET courses of study; aptitude testing; advising students on finding jobs and internships; supervising internships; collecting data on graduates and employment; and facilitating the matching of students and employers for internships and job placement. To do so, the offices could provide individual counseling, hard copy and Internet resources, group seminars, and tours of employers. Since there is no history of guidance and counseling in the KRI, external consultants might be needed to advise the TVET Secretariat on how to develop these services. Over the longer term, teacher-training institutions should offer specific programs to prepare guidance and career counselors.

Implementation Phasing and Priorities

These actions will require significant planning, budgets, management effort, and time. Not everything can be done at once. In Figure 5.2, we offer a suggested phasing of the implementation steps in the near, medium, and long term. In some cases, we show how recommendations can be divided into steps taken at different points in time. Near-term actions are those that would provide the preparation and lay the groundwork for later actions. Medium-term actions are those that begin building and using the structures necessary to meet TVET objectives. Long-term actions are accomplishments to aspire to or those that would further build on the steps in the previous phases.

A Note on Costs

Expanding and upgrading the quality of secondary vocational education in the KRI as outlined here will require additional funding. The main additional costs of vocational education in addition to the costs of general education that would otherwise be provided to students are:

Figure 5.2
Phasing of TVET Development

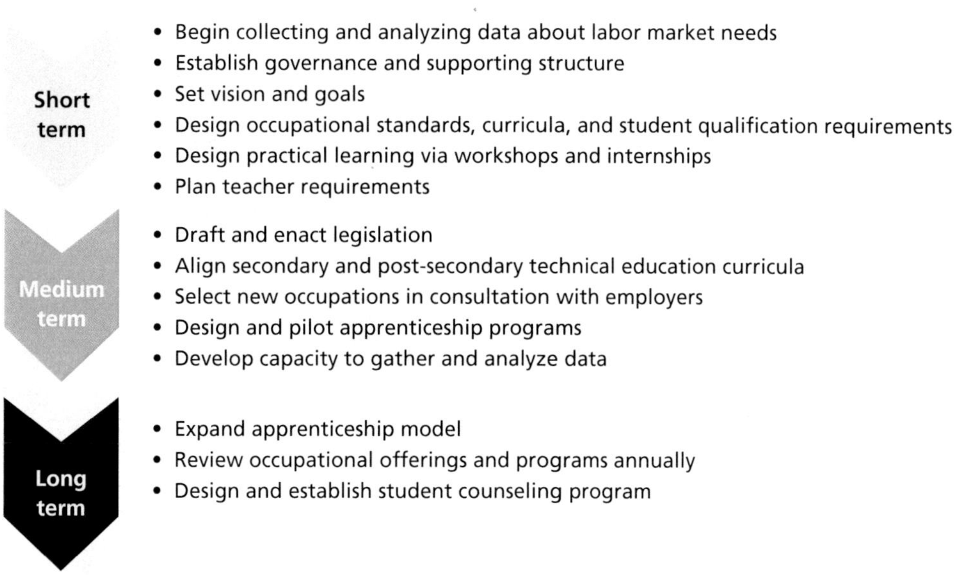

RAND *RR277-5.2*

- The costs of buying and maintaining the occupational equipment needed for on-hand training of vocational students. Such costs can be high, especially for specialized technical equipment.
- The facilities and staffing of the TVET Governing Council and its four supporting offices.
- The development and staffing of a student counseling and guidance capability (although such services would also benefit general education students).
- Upgrading teacher pre-service and in-service training.
- Upgrading occupational standards and curricula.

APPENDIX A

Student Enrollment in Technical and Vocational Education and Training in the KRI

Table A.1
Number and Percentage of Students in Secondary Vocational Education and in Training Centers, by Occupation, 2010–2011

Secondary Vocational (ISCED 3)			Training Centers (ISCED 4)		
Occupation	Number	Percentage	Occupation	Number	Percentage
Trades			Trades		
Automotive	329	4.2	Air conditioning/ refrigerator	154	15.5
Carpentry	186	2.4	Carpentry	82	2.2
Computer	987	12.7	Computer	229	22.9
Electricity	1,340	17.2	Electricity	117	11.7
Electronics	316	4.7	Metal works	49	4.9
Engineering	176	2.3	Sewing	224	22.5
Mechanics	402	5.2	CAB	100	10.0
Metals	157	2.0	–	–	–
Tailoring	43	0.1	–	–	–
Technical drafting	165	2.1	–	–	–
Subtotal	4,101	52.7	Subtotal	955	95.9
Agriculture			Arabic language	24	2.4
Botanical branch	271	3.5	Tourism	17	1.7
Animal branch	72	.9	–	–	–
Agricultural branch	412[a]	5.2	–	–	–
Veterinary	67	.9	–	–	–
Subtotal	822	10.5	–	–	–
Commercial	2,856	36.7	–	–	–
Total	7,779	100.0	Total	996	100.0

SOURCES: MOE and MOLSA.

NOTE: Individual percentages may not add up to subtotal or total because of rounding.

[a] Includes general directorate.

Table A.2
Number and Percentage of Students in Tertiary Technical Education (ISCED 5), by Occupation, 2011–2012

Occupation	Number	Percentage
Trade/technical		
Air conditioning	287	1.0
Civil engineering	207	.7
Conduction	436	1.4
Electricity/power	663	2.2
Electronics	145	.5
Industrial production	135	.4
Material control	107	.3
Mechanical engineering	364	1.2
Mineral and production engineering	220	.7
Oil	159	.5
Structural engineering	221	.7
Surveying	610	2.0
Transportation	118	.4
Subtotal	3,672	12.2
Accounting/administration		
Accounting and financial	4,699	15.6
Administration of law	1,629	5.4
Banking administration	1,647	5.5
Business administration	5,941	19.8
Census and information	395	1.3
Library and information	656	2.2
Marketing	69	.2
Political administration	206	.7
Process technology and administration	463	1.5
Subtotal	15,705	52.3
Agriculture		
Agricultural guidance	109	.4
Food industry	132	.4
Greenhouse	219	.7
Harvesting	220	.7
Horticulture/gardening	150	.5

Table A.2—Continued

Occupation	Number	Percentage
Livestock health	184	.6
Ornamental plants	87	.3
Vegetation protection	270	.9
Vineyard	109	.4
Subtotal	1,480	4.9
IT	2,636	8.8
Medical		
Anesthesia	131	.4
Community and health	381	1.3
Dental hygienist	204	.7
Diagnosis of diseases	880	2.9
Health administration	334	1.1
Maternity and obstetrics	314	1.0
Nursing	1,427	4.7
Pharmacy	378	1.3
Physiotherapy/ therapy	127	.4
Radiology	220	.7
Subtotal	4,396	14.6
Other		
Geography and tourism	229	.8
Journalism	98	.3
Media	821	2.7
Photography	231	.8
Tourism administration	303	1.0
Tourism guidance	327	1.1
Trade	77	.3
Urban planning	63	.2
Subtotal	2,149	7.2

SOURCE: MOHESR.

NOTE: Individual items may not add up to subtotals and totals because of rounding.

APPENDIX B

Occupations and Their Educational Requirements

Table B.1
Definition of Occupations and Educational Requirements

Occupation	Definition	Education and Experience Required
Managers	Professionals who oversee personnel and operations	Tertiary education (ISCED 5)
Professionals	Practically apply extensive theoretical knowledge; increasing stock of knowledge through research; communicating knowledge through teaching	Tertiary education (ISCED 5)
Technicians and associate professionals	Assist in supporting professionals or managers	Post-secondary education (ISCED 4 or 5)
Clerical support workers	General administrative and secretarial work, book-keeping, and specialist-oriented clerical (including financial) duties	Secondary education (ISCED 3)
Service and sales workers	Sell goods and services, accept payment and replenish stocks, provide information to potential clients, and additional services to customers after the point of sale	Secondary education (ISCED 3)
Skilled agricultural, forestry, and fishery workers	Performance of complex physical duties that normally involve initiative, manual dexterity, and other practical skills	Secondary education (ISCED 3)
Craft and related trades workers	Carrying out tasks that require the knowledge and experience of skilled trades or handicrafts. Main tasks consist of extracting raw materials, constructing buildings and other structures, and making various products as well as handicraft goods.	Secondary education (ISCED 3)
Plant and machine operators and assemblers	Operate vehicles and machinery; monitor equipment; product assembly	Secondary or lower (ISCED 3)
Elementary occupations	Mostly routine tasks; use of simple hand-held tools	No formal education required

SOURCES: UK NESS (2007) and ILO (2012).

Bibliography

Abramzon, S., N. Burger, B. Ghosh-Dastidar, P. Glick, K. B. Kumar, F. Perez-Arce, and A. C. Smith (2013), Capacity Building at the Kurdistan Regional Statistics Organization through Data Collection, PR-244-KRG, Santa Monica, CA: RAND.

Al-Hadidi, Duha, and Jordan Ministry of Education (2008), The Development of Education: National Report of the Hashemite Kingdom of Jordan; Inclusive Education: The Way of the Future. Presented to International Conference on Education; 48th; Geneva, 2008. As of April 15, 2013:
http://www.ibe.unesco.org/National_Reports/ICE_2008/jordan_NR08.pdf

Authoring Group Educational Reporting (ed.) (2010), Education in Germany 2010: An Indicator-Based Report Including An Analysis of Education and Migration. Summary of Important Results, p. 14. As of April 15, 2013:
http://www.bildungsbericht.de/daten2010/summary10.pdf

Axmann, M. (2004), "Facilitating Labour Market Entry for Youth Through Enterprise-Based Schemes in Vocational Education and Training and Skills Development," SEED Working Paper No. 48, InFocus Programme on Boosting Employment Through Small Enterprise Development, Job Creation, and Enterprise Department, International Labour Organization, Geneva, Switzerland.

Brown, D., M. Harris, and T. Fletcher (2011), "Reforming the Skills System: Lessons Learned the Hard Way," Institute of Directors and CFE, Leicester and London, United Kingdom.

Cedefop (2012), Thematic Overview for Finland, Practices to Math VET Provision with Skill Needs. As of April 15, 2013:
http://cedefop.europa.eu/EN/Information-services/vet-in-europe-country-reports.aspx

Cedefop's ReferNet (2012). As of April 15, 2013:
http://www.cedefop.europa.eu/EN/Information-services/vet-in-europe-country-reports.aspx

Cedefop (2012), Trends in VET Policy in Europe: 2010–2012, Luxembourg: Publications Office of the European Union.

Center on International Education Benchmarking (2011), South Korea: Overview, Washington DC: National Center on Education and the Economy. As of April 15, 2013:
http://www.ncee.org/programs-affiliates/center-on-international-education-benchmarking/top-performing-countries/south-korea-overview/

Chae, C., and J. Chung (2009), "Pre-Employment VET in Korea in Social Protection and Labour," Discussion Paper No 0921, World Bank.

Chakroun, B. (2003), Innovative Practices in Teacher and Trainer Training in the Mediterranean Region, Turin: European Training Foundation. As of April 15, 2013:
http://www.etf.europa.eu/webatt.nsf/0/C12578310056925BC125701F004D3D86/$file/TTT%20MEDA_03_EN.pdf

Clark, N. (April 2006), "Education in Tunisia," World Education News and Reviews, New York: World Education Services. As of April 15, 2013:
http://www.wes.org/ewenr/PF/06apr/pfpractical_tunisia.htm

Constant, L., S. Culbertson, J. Luoto, and G. Vernez (2012), Assessing Employer Demand for Technical and Vocational Skills in the Kurdistan Region—Iraq, unpublished RAND report.

COSIT, KRSO, The World Bank (2008), Iraq Household Socio-Economic Survey, IHSES: Tabulation Report, 2007.

Culbertson, S., C. Stasz, and G. Vernez (2012), Improving Training in the Kurdistan Region of Iraq: International TVET Policies and Practices, unpublished report, Santa Monica, CA: RAND.

Department of Statistics, Jordan (2011), Tables of Employment and Unemployment, 2011. As of April 17, 2013:
http://www.dos.gov.jo/dos_home_a/main/cd_yb2011/pdf/work.pdf

Education Training Foundation (2011), Torino Process: Compendium of Country Reports, May. As of April 15, 2013:
http://www.etf.europa.eu/web.nsf/pages/Torino_Process_-_compendium_of_country_reports

Education Training Foundation (2010), Education and Business Cooperation Study: Turkey. As of April 15, 2013:
http://www.etf.europa.eu/web.nsf/pages/Education_and_Business_-_Turkey

EFT/WB (2005), Reforming Technical and Vocational Education in the Middle East and North Africa: Experiences and Challenges, Report by the European Training Fund (ETF) and World Bank (WB), Luxembourg: Office for Official Publications of the European Communities, 2006.

El Sawry, K., C. Farr, and S. Newera (2012), Saving Vocational Education in a New Arab World: Arabic Knowledge@Wharton. As of April 15, 2013:
http://knowledge.wharton.upenn.edu/arabic/article.cfm?articleid=2764

Employment, Technical and Vocational Education Training (E-TVET) Fund of Jordan website. As of April 15, 2013:
http://etvetfund.gov.jo/index.php?option=com_content&view=article&id=59&Itemid=68&lang=en

Eurobarometer (2011), Attitudes Toward Vocational Education and Training. Special Report 369, European Commission. As of April 15, 2013:
http://ec.europa.eu/public_opinion/archives/ebs/ebs_369_en.pdf

European Centre for Development of Vocational Training (2008), The Development of National Qualifications Frameworks in Europe, Luxemburg: Office of the European Union.

European Training Foundation/World Bank (ETF/WB, 2005), Reforming Technical and Vocational Education in the Middle East and North Africa: Experiences and Challenges, Report by the European Training Foundation and World Bank, Luxembourg: Office for Official Publications of the European Communities, 2006.

Eurostat (2012), Data files on Turkey. As of April 15, 2013:
http://epp.eurostat.ec.europa.eu/portal/page/portal/statistics/search database

Eurydice Network (2012), Key Data on Education in Europe 2012, Brussels: Education, Audiovisual and Culture Executive Agency. As of April 15, 2013:
http://eacea.ec.europa.eu/education/eurydice/documents/key_data_series/134EN.pdf

Eurydice Network (2011), National System Overview on Education Systems in Europe: Turkey, November 2011. As of April 17, 2013:
https://webgate.ec.europa.eu/fpfis/mwikis/eurydice/index.php/Turkey:Overview

Eurypedia (2012), Germany: Overview. As of April 15, 2013:
https://webgate.ec.europa.eu/fpfis/mwikis/eurydice/index.php/Germany:Overview

Eurypedia (2012), Turkey: Overview. As of April 15, 2013:
https://webgate.ec.europa.eu/fpfis/mwikis/eurydice/index.php/Turkey:Overview

Eurypedia (2012), Turkey: Teachers and Education Staff, 2012. As of April 15, 2013:
https://webgate.ec.europa.eu/fpfis/mwikis/eurydice/index.php/Turkey:Teachers_and_Education_Staff

Federal Office for Professional Education and Technology (OPET) (2011), Vocational Education and Professional Training in Switzerland, Bern, Switzerland: OPET.

Grubb, W. N., R. Sweet, M. Gallagher, and O. Tuomi (2009), OECD Reviews of Tertiary Education—Korea, Paris: OECD Publishing. As of April 15, 2013:
http://www.oecd.org/korea/38092630.pdf

Guthrie, S., C. Holmes, C. Stasz, H. Ertl, E. Watters, L. Villalba-van-Dijk, S. Castle-Clarke, and S. Drabble (2012), Attractiveness of Initial Vocational Education and Training in Europe: What Really Matters, final report to Cedefop, Cambridge: RAND Europe.

Hoeckel, K. (2008), Costs and Benefits in Vocational Education and Training, Paris: OECD.

Hoeckel, K. (2010), Learning for Jobs, OECD Reviews of Vocational Education and Training: Austria, Paris: OECD.

Hoeckel, K., S. Field, and W. N. Grubb (2009), Learning for Jobs, OECD Reviews of Vocational Education and Training: Switzerland, Paris: OECD.

Hoeckel, K., and R. Schwartz (2010), Learning for Jobs. OECD Reviews of Vocational Education and Training: Germany, Paris: OECD. As of April 15, 2013:
http://www.oecd.org/dataoecd/9/6/45668296.pdf

IFF Research Ltd. (2007), United Kingdom National Employer Skills Survey 2007 Mainstage Questionnaire. As of April 15, 2013:
http://employersurveys.ukces.org.uk/Employer%20Survey%20Images/NESS07/NESS%202007%20Main%20Questionnaire.pdf

International Finance Corporation and Islamic Development Bank (2011), Education for Employment: Realizing Arab Youth Potential, Washington, D.C.

International Labour Organization (2008), Skills for Improved Productivity, Employment Growth and Development, Report V, International Labour Conference, 97th Session, Geneva, Switzerland.

International Labour Organization (2010a), "Teachers and Trainers for the Future—Technical and Vocational Education and Training in a Changing World," Report for Discussion at the Global Dialogue Forum on Vocational Education and Training (29–30 September 2010), Geneva, Switzerland.

International Labour Organization (2010b), A Skilled Workforce for Strong, Sustainable, and Balanced Growth: A G20 Training Strategy, Geneva, Switzerland.

International Labour Organization (2012), International Standard Classification of Occupations: Summary of Major Groups. As of April 15, 2013:
http://www.ilo.org/public/english/bureau/stat/isco/isco88/publ4.htm

Investor Information Service for Jordan (2009). Vocational Training in Jordan. As of April 15, 2013:
http://iis-jordan.com/library/634464670448926250.pdf

Jordan Ministry of Education (2008), The Development of Education: National Report of the Hashemite Kingdom of Jordan; Inclusive Education: The Way of the Future, presented at the 48th International Conference on Education, Geneva, 2008. As of April 15, 2013:
http://www.ibe.unesco.org/National_Reports/ICE_2008/jordan_NR08.pdf

Jordan Ministry of Labor (2009), E-TVET Sector Reform, 2009. As of April 15, 2013:
http://www.etvetreform.org/page.php?ID=10&lang=en

Jordan Ministry of Labor (2009), E-TVET Sector Reform. As of April 15, 2013:
http://www.mol.gov.jo/Default.aspx?tabid=281

Jordan Ministry of Labor, National Training and Employment Project (NTEP). As of, April 15, 2013:
http://www.mol.gov.jo/tabid/222/default.aspx

Jordan Vocational Training Corporation, General Information. As of April 17, 2013:
http://images.jordan.gov.jo/wps/wcm/connect/gov/eGov/Government+Ministries+_+Entities/Vocational+Training+Corporation/

Kis, V., M. L. Ferreira, S. Fiel, and T. Zwick (2008), Learning for Jobs, OECD Reviews of Vocational Education and Training: Hungary, Paris: OECD.

Korean Ministry of Education, Science and Technology, Major Policies and Plans for 2011. As of April 15, 2013:
http://english.mest.go.kr/web/40724/en/board/enview.do?bbsId=276&boardSeq=20684&mode=view

Korean Ministry of Education, Science and Technology. Education for the Future: Science and Technology Towards the Future: Overview. As of April 15, 2013:
http://english.mest.go.kr/web/1693/site/contents/en/en_0203.jsp

Kurdistan Region Labor Force Survey (2012).

Kuczera, M., G. Brunello, S. Field, and N. Hoffman (2008), Learning for Jobs, OECD Reviews of Vocational Education and Training: Norway, Paris: OECD.

Kuczera M., V. Kis, and G. Wurzburg (2009), Learning for Jobs, OECD Reviews of Vocational Education and Training: Korea, Paris: OECD.

Kyro, M. (2006), Vocational Education and Training in Finland: Short Description, Cedefop Panorama series; 130, Cedefop (European Centre for the Development of Vocational Training), Luxembourg: Office for Official Publication of the European Communities.

Majcher-Teleon, Agnieszka, and Ummuhan Bardak (2011), Flexicurity Analysis of the Labor Market in Turkey, Torino: Education Training Foundation, March. As of April 15, 2013:
http://www.etf.europa.eu/webatt.nsf/0/1A7DEF4E58F42D41C12579440040803B/$file/Flexicurity_Turkey.pdf

Mayen, G. (ed.), R. Johanson, M. Chemingui, and A. Mustafa, Technical and Vocational Education in Jordan: Areas for Development Cooperation, Luxembourg: European Training Foundation, 2006. As of April 15, 2013:
http://www.etf.europa.eu/web.nsf/(RSS)/C125782B0048D6F6C12571B0002D1640?OpenDocument&LAN=EN

Ministry of Higher Education and Scientific Research (2010), A Roadmap to Quality: Reforming the System of Higher Education and Scientific Research in the Kurdistan Region of Iraq, Erbil: Kurdistan regional Government.

Ministry of Higher Education and Scientific Research (2012), Higher Education Features 2010-11, Tunis: Studies, Planning and Programming Office. As of April 15, 2013:
http://www.mes.tn/anglais/donnees_de_base/depliant10-11_ang.pdf

Mourshed M., D. Farrell, and D. Barton (2013), Education to Employment: Designing a System That Works, McKinsey & Company: McKinsey Center for Government.

National Center for Human Resources Development, Jordan, TVET Indicators. As of April 15, 2013:
http://www.nchrd.gov.jo/Home/tabid/36/language/en-US/Default.aspx

Organization for Economic Co-operation and Development (2008), Education at a Glance 2008: OECD Indicators, Paris: OECD, doi: 10.1787/eag-2008-en

Organization for Economic Co-operation and Development (2010), Learning for Jobs: Synthesis Report of the OECD Reviews of Vocational Education and Training, Paris: OECD.

Organization for Economic Co-operation and Development (2011), OECD Skills Strategy, Paris: OECD.

RAND Survey of Business Establishments (2012).

ReferNet (2011), Finland: VET in Europe—Country Report. As of April 15, 2013:
http://www.cedefop.europa.eu/EN/Information-services/vet-in-europe-country-reports.aspx

Republic of Turkey, Ministry of National Education, Official Statistics Programme, National Education Statistics: Formal Education, 2011-2012. As of April 15, 2013:
http://sgb.meb.gov.tr/istatistik/meb_istatistikleri_orgun_egitim_2011_2012.pdf

Republic of Turkey, Ministry of National Education, Official Statistics Programme (2010), National Education Statistics: Non-Formal Education, 2009-2010. As of April 15, 2013:
http://www.turkstat.gov.tr/Kitap.do?metod=KitapDetay&KT_ID=5&KITAP_ID=38

Republic of Turkey, Ministry of National Education (2012), National Education Statistics: Formal Education, 2011-2012. Official Statistics Programme. As of April 15, 2013:
http://sgb.meb.gov.tr/istatistik/meb_istatistikleri_orgun_egitim_2011_2012.pdf

Schwalje, Wes (2011), "Examining Global Skills Gaps: How Skills Gaps Impact Firm Performance in the Arab World," International Human Resources Conference and Exhibition, Dubai, U.A.E.

Seyfreid, E. (2008), Thematic Studies: Quality and Quality Assurance in Technical and Vocational Education and Training, Luxembourg: Office for Official Publications of the European Communities, European Training Foundation.

Shatz, H. J., L. Constant, J. Luoto, A. C. Smith, S. Abramzon, and P. Glick (2012), Fostering Private-sector Job Growth in the Kurdistan Region—Iraq, PR-266-KRG, Santa Monica, CA: RAND.

Sondergaard, L., and M. Murthi, with D. Abu-Ghaida, C. Bodewig, and J. Rutkowski (2012), Skills, Not Just Diplomas: Managing Education for Results in Eastern Europe and Central Asia, Directions in Development: Human Development, Washington, D.C.: The World Bank.

Stasz, C., D. McArthur, M. Lewis, and K. Ramsey (1990), Teaching and Learning Generic Skills for the Workplace, R-4004-NCRVE/UCB, Santa Monica, CA: RAND.

Stasz, C., K. Ramsey, R. Eden, J. DaVanzo, H. Farris, and M. Lewis (1993), Classrooms that Work: Teaching Generic Skills in Academic and Vocational Settings, MR-169-NCRVE/UCB, Santa Monica, CA: RAND.

Sultana, R. G., and A. Watts, (2007), Comparative Analysis: Career Guidance in the Mediterranean Region, Turin: European Training Foundation. As of April 15, 2013:

http://www.etf.europa.eu/webatt.nsf/0/C12578310056925BC125735D0051273B/$file/NOTE785KJJ.pdf

Sweet, R. (2009), Comparative Analyses: Work-Based Learning Programmes for Young People in the Mediterranean Region, Italy: European Training Foundation. As of April 15, 2013:
http://www.etf.europa.eu/web.nsf/pages/Work-based_learning_programmes_for_young_people_in_the_Mediterranean_region_(MEDA_ETE_regional_project)

The New VTC: Skills Education for the 21st Century (2012), About the Jordan VTC. As of April 15, 2013:
http://www.thenewvtc.com/about-the-jordan-vtc/

TNS Opinion & Social and the Directorate-General Education and Culture, (2011), Attitudes Toward Vocational Education And Training. Special Eurobarometer Report 369, European Commission. As of April 15, 2013:
http://ec.europa.eu/public_opinion/archives/ebs/ebs_369_en.pdf

UK NESS (2007), United Kingdom National Employers Skills Survey 2007 Mainstage Questionnaire, London: United Kingdom: IFF Research, LTD.

UNESCO (2006), Participation in Formal Technical and Vocational Education and Training Programmes Worldwide: An Initial Statistical Study. As of April 15, 2013:
http://www.uis.unesco.org/library/document/formal-technical-vocational-education-training-tvet-2006.eng.pdf

UNESCO-IBE (2008), The Development of Education, National Report 2004–2008, Ministry of Education and Training, Republic of Tunisia. As of April 15, 2013:
http://www.ibe.unesco.org/National_Reports/ICE_2008/tunisia_NR08_efa.pdf

UNESCO-IBE (2011), "Jordan," World Data on Education 2010–2011, 7th Ed, August. As of April 15, 2013:
http://www.ibe.unesco.org/fileadmin/user_upload/Publications/WDE/2010/pdf-versions/Jordan.pdf

UNESCO and ICON Institute (2012), "Potential for Partnership and Collaboration Between Private Sector and TVET Institutions in Kurdistan," Workshop organized by UNESCO Iraq Office and convened at the European Technology and Training Centre (ETTC) in Erbil, July 18, 2012.

UNESCO Institue of Statistics (2012), Education, Statistical Tables, Table 5. As of May 5:
http://stats.uis.unesco.org/unesco/TableViewer/tableView.aspx

UNESCO ISCED (1997), Mappings Republic of Korea Based on the 2008 School Year. As of April 15, 2013:
http://www.uis.unesco.org/Education/ISCEDMappings/Pages/default.aspx

USAID-Iraq (2010), Tijara Provincial Economic Growth Program, Market Assessment Summary: Business Constraints and Opportunities at the Business Enabling Environment and Firm Levels for the Province of Erbil, Iraq, USAID, Washington D.C., March.

USAID-Iraq (2010), Tijara Provincial Economic Growth Program, Market Assessment Summary: Business Constraints and Opportunities at the Business Enabling Environment and Firm Levels in Iraq, USAID, Washington D.C., June.

Vernez, G., S. Culbertson, and L. Constant (2012), Strategic Priorities for Improving Access to Quality Education in the Kurdistan Region—Iraq, PR-1140-KRG, Santa Monica, CA: RAND.

Vivian, D., M. Winterbotham, J. Shury, B. Davies, and S. Constable (2011), UK Employer Skills Survey 2011: First Findings, Rotherham, UK: IFF Research and UK Commission for Employment and Skills.

Watters, E. (2009), Making Initial Vocational Education and Training More Attractive for Learners, Report for European Network on Quality Assurance in Vocational Education and Training (ENQA-VET), European Commission, Directorate General Education and Culture.

World Bank (2010), Stepping Up Skills: For More Jobs and Higher Productivity, Washington, D.C.

World Bank (2011), Iraq Country Profile 2011, Enterprise Survey, Washington, D.C. As of April 15, 2013: http://www.enterprisesurveys.org/Data/ExploreEconomies/2011/iraq#workforce--location.